THE POWER
OF CHOOSING PEACE

REALIZE GOD'S PERFECT LOVE IN YOU

Paul T Cardillo, J.D.

All references to *A Course in Miracles* (ACIM), are to the Third Edition Combined Volume. Mill Valley, CA: Foundation for Inner Peace, 2007.

ISBN: 978-0-578-62184-5
Library of Congress Cataloging-in-Publication Data on file

Printed by Diggy POD, Inc. in the United States of America. First Printing 2019.

Cover Design by Michelle Cardillo
Edited by Sharon Jebens

This book is dedicated to my best friend and wife, Michelle. Thank you for your light, love and encouragement.

Contact: ptcardillo@gmail.com paulcardillo.com

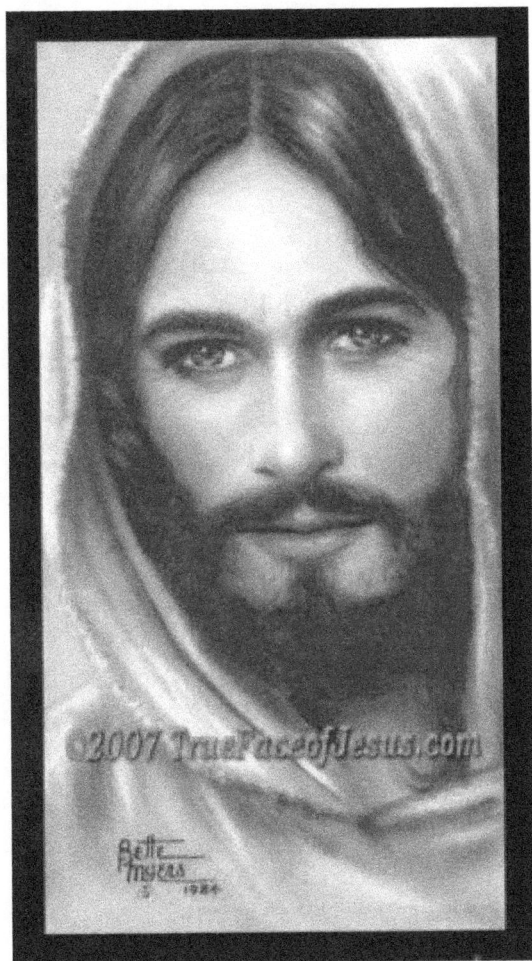

This painting, 'The Masterpiece', is by Bette Myers. It is the face of Christ that appeared to me in 2000, Ft. Lauderdale Florida, at the Hay House Convention.

The Madonna del cardellino or Madonna of the Goldfinch by Rafael c. 1505–1506.

This painting is quite significant to me. My last name, Cardillo, is Sicilian. It means "goldfinch". The goldfinch in Italian Renaissance art is symbolic of the Resurrection.

Table of Contents

THE POWER OF
CHOOSING OF PEACE

THE POWER OF CHOOSING PEACE
Introduction

We are looking for peace and love in a world that is chaotic and threatening. We are yearning for harmony and flow within a world full of twists and turns. We are looking for safety and satisfaction in a world full of security cameras and money changers. We are looking for happiness and connection in a world of loneliness and sadness. We are looking for certainty and abundance in a world that is unpredictable and full of scarcity.

I have experienced the futility of searching for peace in the world. Inevitably, we will all experience something in our life that turns it upside down. Maybe it's a financial failure, a relationship failure, a major illness, an addiction or just plain emptiness. If we pay attention, these disillusionments can actually lead us out of the darkness into the Light of happiness and peace. If looked at through the eyes of our Christ Self, we will see the Light at the end of what seems like an endless tunnel of despair and frustration.

My journey began when my first marriage failed 25 years ago. It was a shock to the happily-ever-after plan that my personal, ego-self had set in motion. When it failed, I fell into confusion and fear. *Disillusioned* best describes the feeling. I was Catholic, and divorce was frowned upon. After the divorce, I had custody of my young daughters, no money and spiritual confusion. The Catholic church was of little help. I was not permitted to receive communion until my marriage was annulled. I think that was the icing on the cake of my spiritual confusion. In my time of greatest need, why was I not permitted to receive, what I was taught to believe was the very "body and blood" of Jesus. What kind of loving religion would tell me I was not worthy to receive Jesus?

My disillusionment set me off on a Spirit-driven journey to find what I now know as the Presence of the Peace and Love of God. I found it by following the carefully laid Plan of Light that Jesus came to teach us. The Plan has led me to teachers along the way who held my hand through fear and uncertainty.

Eventually, after Jesus appeared to me at a Hay House Convention in Ft. Lauderdale and gifted me with a painting, my spiritual awareness began to expand and deepen. The Holy Spirit and Jesus, through their teachings in *A Course in Miracles*, opened my awareness to the Light of God, our Source.

Once we choose the purpose and guidance of the Holy Spirit, our path is made smooth. Miracles and synchronicities lead the way in our family and work lives. Present trust in the Holy Spirit--the Spirit of God's Perfect Love and Peace-- solves all problems. Worries and concerns are replaced by the sweet safety of grace in the midst of our daily lives so full of chaos.

When I was a law student, I was taught to represent my clients by some of the very best lawyers in Texas. For the past thirty years I have represented clients who could not speak for themselves. My practice has included injuries, social security disability, criminal defense and divorces. Our legal system, though the best in the world, lacks enough compassion and love. It is a system full of fear and anxiety. As a lawyer I have done my best to calm my clients' fears and guide them through to a peaceful resolution.

So that I would be fully prepared to help the reader of this book, I have spent the last 20 years of my life, while still practicing law and raising a family, looking for the answer to the healing and relieving of misery, suffering, depression and pain. I have a library full of books of every conceivable spiritual path known to man, including the Bible. Many were very helpful. Many were not. The Bible is helpful in that for many of us it is our first exposure to the love of Jesus. But the Bible also sends severely mixed messages of love and fear, sin, suffering and guilt. The Love of God is incompatible with the fear attributed to God. So, from the Bible, we should assimilate the Love, but look beyond the fear to the Light.

The only book that has answered every question I have asked and met every fear that has come my way is *A Course in Miracles*. For those of you who may not know, *A Course in Miracles* is a book of Jesus' words dictated to and written down by Helen Schucman Ph.D., during a seven-year period from 1965 to 1972. Helen, at the time of taking down the words of this book, was a professor of medical psychology at Columbia University in New York. The most complete and accurate account of the process of Helen's taking down Jesus' words is best described in *Absence from Felicity* by Kenneth Wapnick and the Foundation for Inner Peace. Suffice it to say though, *A Course in Miracles* is a book of Jesus' words that have the power to bring us home to peace.

Since Jesus physically appeared to me, I have been being prepared to step out to teach the Law of Love and Peace. In my personal life, I have dealt with the challenges of finances, relationship and sickness that we all face sooner or later. I know the threat these challenges present to our peace. And most importantly, with the guidance of Jesus and the Holy Spirit, I know how to help replace threat, suffering, uncertainty and depression with Love, through the Power of Peace that we all have. Our Choice for Peace *is* Power. God created nothing other than Peace and Love. All thought, other than the Thought of Peace, is false power. We have the sacred option Choose the Power of Peace now. Peace loves Love. Love loves Peace.

This book is for those who suffer in silence. It is for those who think that the Love and Peace of God has abandoned them, leaving them stranded in a lonely world of fear and threat. It is for everyone who longs for peace and tranquility. This book is for those who are not happy in relationships, body, finances and purpose. We have suffered enough, and we just want peace. Through the inspiration of Jesus and the Holy Spirit, I know how to help remember the Power of Peace in each of us that results in greater joy, happiness and a feeling of well-being. Only Perfect Love exists. Peace clears the way.

This book is not written from the isolation of a mountain top. I have not left the world of work and family. I am a 30-year lawyer with vast experience. I have a wife, four children and bills to pay. I know the problems, worries and challenges to peace in our lives. I have experienced foreclosure, divorce and my wife's cancer. I wash dishes and pay bills. I teach *A Course in Miracles* and work out at the YMCA. And, at the start of this journey, Jesus appeared and gave me a painting of the face of Christ. I know the rubber, the road and where they meet. I know it all is illusion, and yet we must deal with it.

I know the Power of Choosing Peace and how it looks through and beyond what seem to be obstacles to the awareness of Perfect Love's Presence. It is my prayer that the inspired words of this book will help bring us all back into the Kingdom of Heaven.

This is not a book about withdrawing from the world to go sit on a mountain top. It is about finding the mountain top within your mind and sitting "there" in the Peace of God. When you are finished with this book, it is my hope that you will feel less misery, less anxiety, less suffering and more love, joy, peace and happiness.

Neither is this book about manifesting. *The script is written.* We have tried to manifest things in the world, perhaps with what seems like success. The attempt at manifestation is the attempt to find happiness and the feeling of fulfillment in the dream world. At some point along the way to awakening (remembering the Truth), we accept the glorious fact that we are Spirit, and the only "manifestation" worthwhile is the alignment with the Will of God. Align with the Kingdom of Heaven, and all that is needed is provided. Vision boards are of the dream world. The ego dream will even make it look like we manifest at times. Soon we find that the failure at manifestation in relationships, careers and experiences in the world will eventually trigger us to ask for a better way to find peace. Affirmations, attending church every Sunday, vision boards and tapping our temples-- although helpful--have not brought sustained peace and happiness.

The dream world that appears before our eyes is there to divert our attention from the Kingdom of Heaven. The appearance-world is simply a world made of images that flash within the human mind, or what we may call our human awareness. These appearances are pictures of concepts of opposites made up by the ego-false mind to ensure conflict. Conflicting concepts were not created by God's Mind of Love. Jesus, in *A Course in Miracles*, tells us that they are not "there". And yet, they sure do seem to be "there" right in front of our eyes. This is the dilemma. Appearances seem to be "there," and they capture our attention all day until it is time to sleep. Then when we sleep, we find that the dream world is even there in our sleep.

We are taught by the world that the images we see with our physical eyes while we are awake during the day is the "real" world. We are then taught that when we close our eyes to sleep at night, we enter a dream world that is not real and that the images we see in the sleep time are hallucinations the sleeping mind conjures up. Then, after we wake from the at-night-sleep-world, we are taught that we wake to the "real" world. We open our eyes, yawn, stretch, take a shower, dress the kids, eat breakfast and then off to work to make money so that we can keep repeating this pattern until it's time to die. Of course, all mixed in there are vacations, Botox, college tuition, divorce, cancer, foreclosures, doctor visits, insurance payments, overdue rent and mortgage payments, car accidents, taxes, traffic tickets and oh my, lions and tigers and bears!

We look for relief from our anxiety and misery to astrologers, priests, alcohol, antidepressants, yogis, sweat tents, churches, temples, confession, religions, massage, past−life regression, vision boards, phycologists, snake handling, deep breathing, drugs, vegetarianism, divine feminine and masculine, totem poles and gurus on the Ganges!

Although these can be of some value as steppingstones, we soon find that they only have a temporary, topical effect. They are band− aids. We can now cross them off our lists in the quest for peace.

The appearance world is a place of constant and continuing threat. We are threatened by the world with the possibility of sickness, accidents, poverty, loss of job, death, loss of a spouse or partner, world war and crime. There is no Peace *in* the world. Locks can be made stronger, video cameras can be installed, insurance can be in place, along with 401ks and retirement pensions. And guess what happens anyway? We seem to die. Shouldn't this at least cause us to ask, "Why am I doing all this? What is it for? What is this world? Where or how can I find the Peace of God?"

Those were my questions years ago, and it is my focus today. I have been blessed with much help along the way. You picked up this book because it is your destiny to wake up to the Love and Peace of God. As Jesus has told us, the Kingdom of Heaven is spread out before us, but we don't see it. Many years ago, I asked in my heart to see it, to feel it and to remember it. It is my prayer that you, too, will begin to remember who you really are and return Home to the Light, Peace, and Love of God.

"I cannot go without you, for you are part of me."
(Jesus, ACIM, in The Song of Prayer)

Paul Cardillo, October 2019

For what appears to hide the face of Christ
is powerless before His majesty and disappears before His holy sight.
— ACIM Chapter 31 VIII.4

1

JESUS APPEARS

WHEN JESUS APPEARED TO ME at a Hay House convention in Fort Lauderdale, Florida almost 20 years ago, life for me changed completely. I was drawn to the Hay House Convention because I was impressed and inspired by Dr. Wayne Dyer. He was the keynote speaker at the convention, and I was eager to hear him speak live. Little did I know that my admiration of Wayne Dyer would result in Jesus physically appearing to me. Jesus spoke no verbal words to me at that time. Yet, even without a word, the smile and peace on his face spoke to me in a way no words ever could. His eyes, so full of light and love, left no doubt of his request of me.

In the past twenty years, he and the Holy Spirit have guided me in my personal life in ways unimaginable. When Jesus appeared to me, I was a young lawyer, primarily on my own raising two small daughters, Brittney and Megan, from a previous marriage. My new (and current) wife, Michelle, was pregnant with our first child, Phoenix. It was a very turbulent, challenging time in my life. I was looking for peace that no church or religion could provide, which is why, in looking back, I was led to the Hay House Convention.

My wife and I had wandered into James Van Praagh's presentation quite by chance. I don't think I knew who he was at the time. I believe it was the second day of the convention. Michelle and I had attended Wayne Dyer's opening night presentation the previous night. before. We had also attended Doreen Virtue's presentation, and we had an empty timeslot to fill. Mr. Van Praagh's bio and presentation synopsis sounded like it could be interesting, so we wandered in. As we walked in, I was struck by the large size of the room and how many people were already seated. At that very instant, I heard a quiet voice within me say very clearly, "you will speak to much larger audiences than this."

I can't even begin to explain how odd it was for me to hear these words. I was simply there at the Hay House Convention looking for answers. I was very new to anything other than traditional Catholic Christianity. I had begun reading *A Course in Miracles* and had read Wayne Dyer, Deepak Chopra, Joel Goldsmith and Paramahansa Yogananda over the previous two or three years. But I had no intention to speak to audiences. I remember thinking how crazy it was to entertain the thought of speaking to people about Spirituality. I was trying to understand it and had no intention to teach what I did not understand. I simply wanted peace in my life as a husband, father and lawyer.

Apparently, Jesus had other plans for me. As part of his presentation, James Van Praagh had us turn to someone in the audience that we did not know. I think the point of the exercise was to "see spiritually" as James said it was a gift or talent that we all have to some degree. I turned around to a man behind me. He was a big, middle-aged man with blonde hair. We spoke briefly. He was from New Jersey. The lights were then dimmed. We were instructed to simply do our best to drop our judgments and expectations of the way we see and to simply relax our vision and gaze. Even though it sounded a bit out of my wheelhouse as a logical lawyer, I surrendered to the experience.

Within a few moments the big blonde man from New Jersey was no longer sitting across from me. Instead, there was a man with long hair, a beard and a hood with a pleasant, peaceful smile. This bearded, hooded man did not verbally speak to me. His eyes were intently full of light and peace. His smile gave me a feeling of reassurance and certainty of purpose. The appearance of this man lasted less than a minute, but I was riveted by the experience. After the lights came back up, we all traded stories about what we each had experienced. My wife had had seen German Shepherd dogs around her partner, which made sense to him because his two German Shepherds had recently died. I told my experience to my partner from New Jersey. He could not relate the bearded, hooded man to anything that was going on in his life. 'Oh well,' I thought, then I had no idea of what I had just experienced. Shortly thereafter, the presentation ended, and we walked out into the convention hall to the area where the writers and artists were selling their books and artwork.

As we walked past an author's booth, out of the corner of my eye to my left, I saw a painting on the wall of the booth. I was riveted and could not turn away from the painting. It was the exact face of the man with the long hair, beard and hood who had just appeared to me 15 minutes before. As I stood there staring at the painting, the author who was selling his books at this booth, Joe Crane, came quickly over to me and asked what I knew about the painting. At first, I did not respond. But he kept insisting that I knew something. Finally, I related my experience to him and his wife, who had also come over to greet me. After briefly describing my experience to him, he was so excited. He explained that he was given the painting of Jesus by Joanne Macko who is a gifted angel artist in the Chicago area. Joanne (who did not paint the Jesus painting) gave Joe the painting to take to Ft. Lauderdale to hang in his booth. She said that Spirit was insistent that the painting had to go with Joe to the Hay House Convention. She did not know why; she just knew it had to be there.

The Cranes' excitement was further compounded by the fact that they saw that I had a remarkable resemblance to the Jesus painting. They asked if they could photograph me with the painting, and I agreed. The photo was sent to Joanne Macko. Skipping over lots of detail, I was invited to speak at Joanne's convention in the Chicago area several months later. Now, over twenty years later, many miracles and synchronicities have happened. I have done my best to fill this book with stories that will give you faith that peace is possible regardless of the circumstances in which you find yourself.

This Jesus Painting, (reproduced in the first pages of this book) the 'Masterpiece' by Bette Myers, has been a miracle for me. (see the painting and "my story" at www.truefaceofjesus.com) It accelerated my awakening to who I am. It set me on a path of Truth that has become my passion to share. The healing of the mind and the return to the Peace of Heaven is achievable, and in fact, inevitable for all of us.

While Christianity can be full of loving and well – intentioned people, it stops short of delivering Jesus's true message. I was raised Catholic. Unfortunately, the Catholic church places a heavy emphasis on the concepts of sin, guilt, fear and ritual--all of which removed me from the Real Peace of God.

It is my hope and prayer that my story will inspire the withdrawal of reliance on what has been taught about sin, guilt, and fear. Jesus has nothing at all to do with any of those concepts, other than to tell us to drop them. He would tell us to unclench our grasp on them and let them go. He did not live his life to demonstrate sin or guilt or fear or sacrifice and suffering. His name has been associated with all of those. He says it is time to shred those false associations.

He lived his life according to our Creator's Plan of Love and Light and Peace. He invites us to follow in his footsteps down the path he has so carefully lit up for us. We can absolutely trust him. He knows the way Home to Heaven. He knows the Plan of Light; he knows God's Plan of Love. He is the first one to have completed his part in the Plan perfectly. His blood did not "save" us. Eating a piece of bread in church, in-and-of-itself, does not "save" us. Jesus tells us that the aim of *A Course in Miracles* is to remove and undo the blocks in our mind that interfere with our awareness that only the Love of God is Present and only the Love of God is Real. He explains that nothing other than the Love of God within us exists at all. Fear, not being the Love of God, does not exist and has no power to make us sad, worried, anxious, depressed or angry. When we realize the Power of Peace lies within us *now*, Love is all that will remain.

Jesus, with the Holy Spirit, is the guiding force in my life. He speaks to and through me, as he is available to everyone. He inspires my thoughts and moves me to walk in his footsteps. Jesus was and is the demonstration of the Love of God. And while he was a Son of God, he, as a man, was not the "only" Son of God. If that were true, then everyone else, at best, would be adopted children of God. And that is not true.

It is my hope that this book will encourage you to sit up, stand up and in the Light, to wake up and open your spiritual eyes to see and *feel* the truth of God's Love in your own life, right here, right now. It is my hope that through my life experiences, you will better understand that the work to be done here in the dream world of time is to overlook, to look "past" and beyond the appearance world to the Peace of Heaven. This is what *A Course in Miracles* calls "forgiveness." Jesus encourages us to stop giving believability and credibility to what we see with the human eye. We can wake up to the feeling, the absolute real feeling, of the Peace and Love of God. It is the only Power that God created. But there is stuff to get out of our way. Our choosing peace will lead us there.

When my wife had cancer about 6 months ago, it rattled me more than a bit. As I will elaborate more on in this book, Jesus spoke very clearly to me about how to handle the fear thoughts that arose. At one point, I asked him for the thought he held in his mind during the extreme circumstances of his crucifixion. He woke me up very early one morning to answer my question with these crystal-clear words:

"I Know Peace," he said. And then there was silence. But I wanted more. He must have held more in his mind. Then he spoke the same words again and added nothing to them: **"I Know Peace."** The sacred silence that followed his words was the most important part of his words, for there was *nothing else* to say. The sacred silence was the exclamation point. He wants us to know peace, for there is nothing else to know. In Peace, we know the Perfect Love of God. He knew the Power of Peace.

Each one of us has a choice to make. No one can make this choice for us, and we are making it each moment of our earthly lives. The choice--the only real choice-- is to choose to remember the Truth of God's Peace. Or, we can choose to continue to believe the lie that we separated from God's Perfect Love and fell from His Grace, which will unnecessarily perpetuate misery, sickness, anxiety and suffering. When we choose the Peace of Love, we have set in motion the only Power that Is. We can trust God's Peace to smooth our way.

We must keep in mind that this choosing of peace is not the choosing of the end of wars or better life circumstances that we all naturally desire. Rather, it is a communing with and in the Light of

God without any desire but to rest in His Present Peace. Therein lies the Power of Peace. We let God cover us in Light and Love, and we do nothing. We hold no thought that would interfere with His Care for us. Then we trust that the Power of Peace has already walked before us and has resolved all matters that concern us.

We have repeated several times before that you
but make a journey that is already done
–ACIM Lesson 169

2

FINDING OUR WAY HOME

THE MYTHICAL FALL from grace in the Garden of
Eden for eating an apple is the story that traditional
religion would have us believe. To believe that story is
to believe God has the ability to carry and harbor anger.
Really? God Is Perfect Love Only. Love is Peace. The
fact that God is only Love completely and totally
eviscerates and eliminates any possibility that our
Creator would deem us as sinners and doom us to a life
of struggle, strife, misery and death. This story of
original sin is a story made up to encourage a belief in
guilt and unworthiness. It is a deceptive story that is
ignorantly perpetuated by traditional religious dogma in
an effort to maintain separation from God's Love. The
false voice of the ego that perpetuates the fear dream
wants us to be afraid of God's punishment for our
"guilt". Common sense causes us to ask how in the
world would I be guilty if some guy named Adam ate an

apple eons ago? Explain the connection to me. And if Jesus's blood shed vicariously "saved" us, then why does most of the world, including Christians, still act like knuckleheads?

Yes, I know, that sounds like the opposite of what we should be teaching in the churches and in the temples. To teach that we are born in sin and separated from God and that Jesus is the only Son of God IS the opposite of truth. Jesus is in fact the way shower. He is the example we are to follow. He shows us the way back to heaven. And he will be the first to say, and does say, we were all created in the Light of God as brothers and sisters in the Light of Love. Jesus would never ever want us to believe that he was the "Only Son of God".

Jesus tells us in *A Course in Miracles, Clarification of Terms*, 5. "*Jesus-Christ*":

"The name of *Jesus* is the name of one who was a man but saw the face of Christ in all his brothers and remembered God".

Each choice we make in life carries with it all the consequences and effects that are inherent in, or built into, and are part of that particular choice. We are always choosing love or fear, heaven or hell, God or the ego. Always--no matter what it may seem we are choosing between--it is always between peace or chaos. Much like ordering food in a restaurant, if we choose to order the steak and lobster, a vegetable and bread come along with it. If we order the spaghetti and meatballs, salad will arrive on our table as well. If we choose to jump in the ocean, we will get wet. If we choose to lick a frozen metal pole in the middle of a Pittsburgh winter, our tongue will get stuck.

So it is when choose the Power of Peace. Peace, Love and the remembrance of our eternal Life with and in God, arrives on our table. When we choose to continue to make the choice to believe the deception of being apart from, or separated from the Presence of Peace, the Love of God, we will experience misery, suffering, despair, disappointment, anger, anxiety, depression and death. These dark and dreary feelings and experiences will arrive at the table of our lives.

We have a choice to make. Do we want happiness? Or do we want depression? Do we want Heaven, or do we want to continue to wallow in hell? The choice is ours to make. No one but ourselves can make that choice. I encourage us all to make the choice to be happy. The Kingdom of Heaven waits for us to make this choice. Jesus' words throughout *A Course in Miracles* and in the Bible are clear:

Seek first the Kingdom of Heaven and all else that you need will be provided.

Jesus loved to tell stories. He used these parables to light up what he was trying to explain. I will relate stories, or parables in this book. Now 60 years old, I realize that the value of my life on earth is that of a parable. The story of Paul, grandson of Joseph and

Mary, Joseph and Jane, son of Peter and Mary, brother to Peter, Mary Jane, Matthew, Mark, Luke, John and David. Husband of Michelle, father of Brittney, Megan, Phoenix and Kira. Son, father, husband, friend, dishwasher, payer of bills and lawyer.

This is the story of how one prodigal son slowly, very slowly, by small degrees, woke up to the understanding that he had wandered into the dream of being separate and apart from the Perfect Love of God, the Creator of all that is and ever shall be. It the parable of one son slowly realizing that the dreamworld of death, sickness, poverty and misery holds nothing of any value whatsoever in and of itself. None. Zero. Zilch. The only value that the dream story can hold is that of healing our hypnotized mind from the false guilt associated with the belief that we have broken away from the Kingdom of Perfect Peace and Happiness.

The story of Paul is that of finding that the Truth in *A Course in Miracles* is the actual roadmap home to the peace of heaven, back to the Father's house after many miserable trips into the insanity of the dreamworld we call earth. *A Course in Miracles* holds within its written words the Light that Is the Kingdom to which we all long to return. This return that we long for is really the awakening of the memory that each and every one of us holds within. It is the memory of eternal peace, within which is happiness so deep and so profound, that we cannot with our human minds even come close to imagining. Peace has the Power to transcend the illusions of the appearances.

29

We can indeed Remember. The Kingdom, our Home, is here now waiting for us to recall it. It is Here Now. Now it is Here. Be still. I assure you that it is Here for us to feel and see.

In the Gospel of Thomas, we have the hidden words that the living Jesus spoke. The Gospel of Thomas holds 114 "Sayings" that Jesus said. As Jesus spoke these words, they were written down by Didymos Judas Thomas, at or near the time they were actually spoken.

Saying (3)

Jesus says:

If those who lead you say to you: 'look, the kingdom is in the sky!' then the birds of the sky will precede you. If they say to you: 'it is in the sea', then the fishes will precede you.
Rather the kingdom is inside of you and outside of you When you come to know yourselves you will be known, and you will realize that you are the children of the living Father.
But if you do not come to know yourselves, then you exist in poverty, and you are poverty.

Saying (59), Jesus says:

"Look for the Living One while you are alive, so that you will not die and then seek to see him. And you will not be able to see him."

30

It is my hope that your journey out of this nightmare
will be accelerated by my experiences. I have in fact,
very literally, *lived A Course in Miracles.* Without
question, without doubt, without hesitation and without a
look back, I can tell you, with great joy, that *A Course
in Miracles* will take you by the hand and lead you back
to remembering the Peace of God. There will be starts,
stops and setbacks in our peace. I have had many, so
many. But ultimately, if we stick with it, the *Course* will
cause us to remember that we are the Miracle of God,
that we are in fact the Peace and Love of the Creator of
All Creation. The Holy Spirit and Jesus are with us now
this very moment asking us to open our hearts and
minds to the freedom that is ours if we truly want the
Peace and Love of God above all else. But we have to
desire it. We have to want to wake up to peace and
happiness in the same measure that a drowning man
wants to rise to the surface of the water. The wanting
and desiring is not an effort of intellect and human
might. Rather the effort is that of a steady, quiet focus
upon the goal of remembering the Truth of who we are.
It is a fixation, to the exclusion of all else, on our
Present Trust in the Perfect Love of God to make good
on the promise that *"this day you shall be with me in
Paradise".*

3

REMEMBER LOVE

PRETENDING TO NO LONGER KNOW something that we know is called 'denial.' Denying, or purposely "forgetting" something we know, doesn't mean *what* we know is gone. It remains "there" to be remembered by choosing to do so. Most importantly, we can't forget something unless at one point we knew it. Right?

ACIM Chapter 10. Sec. II

Unless you know something you cannot dissociate it. Knowledge must precede dissociation, so that dissociation is nothing more than a decision to forget. What has been forgotten (Perfect Love and Peace) then appears to be fearful, but only because the dissociation is an attack on truth. You are fearful because you have forgotten. And you have replaced your knowledge by an awareness of dreams because you are afraid of your dissociation, not of what you have dissociated. When

*what you have dissociated is accepted (Perfect Love
and peace of God), it ceases to be fearful.*

Fear consequently and constantly, knocks at the door of
our minds in an effort to destroy our peace. In the
absence of fear there is peace. One of the keys to
removing the upsetting charge we feel from fear, which
is the denial of Love and Peace, is explained by Jesus:

ACIM Chapter 11. Sec. III

*Fear and love are the only two emotions of which you
are capable. One is false, for it was made out of denial,
and denial depends on the real belief in* **what** *is denied
for its own existence.*
*By interpreting fear correctly as a positive affirmation
of the underlying belief (LOVE) it masks, you are
undermining its perceived usefulness by rendering it
(fear) useless.*

Jesus is clearly telling us that the emotion of fear is not
a creation of God. He is clearly saying that fear is the
emotion that hides the presence of love. We have
hidden love in the very last place we would look. If we
lift the cover from fear, love will arise. The last thing
fear wants us to do is to realize that love is hidden in
fear. It is like thinking that there is a poisonous snake
inside a basket. We are afraid to lift the lid of the basket
because we are afraid the snake will bite us. So we
don't lift the lid. Instead, we turn away.

Fear should be a trigger for us. We can use it as a trigger to help us remember love which removes the seeming power of fear. When fear arises, we can say to ourselves with a smile, "Oh that's right, Jesus says that fear is really my denial of love. And I know that to deny love, I must know love, because I can deny only something known. So, I must know love and peace only. I choose now to remember what fear is trying to deny. I choose love and peace."

We can absolutely, positively remember our Creator. We have temporarily forgotten Peace and Love. As we hold Peace and Love in awareness, we will remember God. We were introduced to God when God created us out of His Divine Mind of Love. In a Holy Instant of Love, we were created as a perfect idea of Love in the Mind of God. God smiled, and we smiled, and we laughed together. After we stopped laughing, God introduced Himself with a hug. "Hi", God said, "Welcome to the Kingdom of Perfect Peace, Love and Joy. It's all yours," the Creator said with a smile, "it's all yours, My Love".

We know Love and Peace. We know God. *A Course in Miracles* is a very powerful approach to God. We will remember because we long for peace and joy. Remember that fear is the denial of love and peace. Then choose Love. Choose Peace.

We have no knowledge of fear. It is illusion. Fear is hallucination. We only can know what God Knows. Good thing! We seem to "see" and "feel" fear. But we can let it go. It is not knowledge. And because our Mind only holds what we think with God, we have the power to dismiss it.

In the Bible, Jesus dismisses Satan simply by saying, "Get thee behind me, Satan."

In the Wizard of Oz, the wicked witch is royally pissed at Dorothy for dropping a house on her sister. She is so angry, she gets all up in the face of Dorothy and threatens her. Glinda the Good Witch of the North is standing right there and isn't ruffled at all by the threat. In fact, Glinda just smiles, waves her off and says, "Be gone, or someone will drop a house on you, too." Glinda is just like the Holy Spirit. She sees right through the threat, right through the blowhard fear. Glinda, like the Holy Spirit she represents in the Land of Oz, isn't the least bit fooled by fearful threats. "Be gone," she says. "You have no power here." We, in the dream of death that we hallucinate, can also say to fear, "Be gone. You have no power here. I have chosen love and peace. "

I recall in the beginning stages of my spiritual journey, one of my early mentors reminded me to use Jesus' words of "Get thee behind me, Satan" as a way of bringing me into alignment with both Jesus and the Truth. It was a tool I used to bring relief from whatever fearful problem was confronting me. These words would calm me down and bring a sense of peace. It can be especially effective when we picture Jesus standing there and speaking these words right along with us.

Then we Trust that we are not alone because it is a fact that Jesus is right there with us every step of the way.

ACIM LESSON 276. The Word (Holy Thought) is given me to speak.

What is the Word of God? "My Son (Holy Creation) is pure and Holy as Myself." Thus, did God become the Father of the Son he loves, for thus he was created. This is the Word His Son did not create with Him, because in this His Son was born. Let us accept His Fatherhood, and all is given us. Deny we were created in His Love and we deny our (Holy) Self, to be unsure of Who we are, of Who our Father is, and for what purpose we have come. And yet we need but acknowledge Him Who gave His Word to us in our creation, to remember Him and so recall our (Holy) Self.

When we chose, for a very teeny, tiny spec of a fraction of an instant, to "forget to remember" that only Love Is, the dream world of love and not love, peace and not peace, flashed across our minds. When we wondered out of innocent curiosity, "What would a world be like without the perfect Peace of God? we also knew that the very question was laughable. It's impossible for a world that is not the perfect Peace of God to exist. Thus, the only way "in" to the dream world of not-peace was to "remember not to laugh" at the idea. Remembering not to laugh was the same as the agreement to take it seriously and to therefore give the idea "value." Along with "valuing" the notion of a world

36

separate from, or not part of the Perfect Peace of Heaven, came the skill of memory that we chose to apply to the false fantasy world of misery that arose and disappeared in an instant. In fact, the length of time it took to type the preceding sentence was a longer time than the "life span" of the world we seem to see in our memory in our minds. In the very instant that the false idea arose, it was gone, corrected and healed by the Love of God, the Holy Spirit. It is gone. The dream world is gone. But we seem to still see it by using the skill of remembering it because we are afraid to forget it and let the false dream go.

We are actually afraid to "remember to laugh at it" because we have a sense of false guilt and doom associated with remembering the present, "the only time there is." So, we continue NOT to laugh at the dream world images and figures. We continue to value it. Why in the heck would we be fearful of laughing at the events, problems, death, emotions, suffering and insanity of the dream world?

Here is why. Here is the answer. We are afraid, subconsciously, at a very deep level, that if we even entertain the thought that the world we see is only an idea, an hallucination in our mind, we will be left without a "defense" to the memory of the truth of who we are, which is pure Perfect Love. The ego, or personal mind voice, that has convinced "us" that "it" is us, planted a deep false belief seed, which we accepted, that to remember the Love of God would be a bad or scary thing. Why? The ego, the false personal self-voice said we are guilty for betraying God by even having the tiny idea of a world that does not include the perfection of heaven. So, the hallucinatory voice encouraged us to lock into the dream world with all the power of our faith. We placed all our faith in the dream world as the replacement or substitute for the Presence of God. This faith is so powerful and locked in that we now seem to have no memory of God. We have become convinced that if we remember God, "He" will destroy us. So it's best to keep "remembering not to laugh." We are actually afraid to leave the theater of the fear dream even though the doors are open. The fear dream is a memory we keep playing in our minds because it keeps us preoccupied with problems and drama so as not to remember the Perfect Peace of Love.

Sounds crazy doesn't it? That's because it is. The Holy Spirit and Jesus are constantly and quietly trying to get us to listen to the Loving Voice for God. Yet, because we are insanely afraid to remember that we are Love, we defiantly stick our fingers in our ears and pretend we can't hear Jesus and the Holy Spirit tell us of God's eternal Love for us. We keep our minds preoccupied with plans to decorate, excessive trips, rearranging furniture, excessive exercise, other people's problems, our own dramas, gossip, political causes, complaints of unfairness and grievances.

ACIM Lesson 8 My mind is preoccupied with past thoughts (the dream images)

…. No one really sees anything. He sees only his thoughts projected outward (onto the screen of your mind that seems to be a "world").

Of course, it is all a lie that we accepted. When we remember God, we are released.

It is much like one of my favorite movies *"What Dreams May Come"*, with Robin Williams. That movie had a huge spiritual impact on me. Basically, Robin Williams' character, Chris, is killed in a car accident leaving his shocked and devastated wife. Previous to his death, both of their young children were killed in a car accident. For some reason, she felt that both accidents were her fault, causing her to live with crushing guilt. They had a very loving and wonderful life together that was shattered when their children died. After Robin Williams' character died, his wife became very depressed and despondent. As spirit, he stays around her, whispering that he still loves her. She feels his presence, but it's not enough. She shortly thereafter commits suicide and ends up in what is depicted as the hell of guilt. Chris then makes his way into her hell to save her from an eternity of wallowing in guilt. She seems catatonic as Chris does his best to wake her from her false guilt. Finally, with simple words of forgiveness of grievances of their lives together and his pure unending love for her, her eyes light up, and she remembers how much they love each other and that they always have been together and always will. The love never ends. It is all a dream, and they realize they can dream a happy dream.

Why do we seem to see and experience the dream? If it's "not there," why do we see it? Again, the answer is because we keep choosing to remember it so that we don't remember Perfect Love.

That's dumb. Why in the world would we continue to choose to play it over and over and over again in our imagination? Here is the short answer. Again, because it distracts and engages us.

But why would we want to continue to remain preoccupied with and distracted by memories of a world that does not exist? Here is the answer again. Because we are afraid to remember Truth, to remember the Love of God.

ACIM, Chapter 28 I Present Memory

" *This world was over long ago. The thoughts that made it are no longer in the mind that thought of them and loved them for a little while. The miracle but shows the past is gone and has no effects. Remembering a cause can but produce illusions of its presence, not effects.*

···." *Memory, like perception, is a skill made up by you to take the place of what God gave in your creation.* "(*perfect peace, happiness and love)*

Ok, you have to agree that to continue to try to blot out the memory of Perfect Love is the same as beating yourself with a hammer and pretending to like it. The world of religions, in general, have taught us that we need to fear God because we have sinned and are sinners. We are guilty. Religion says when Adam ate the apple, we all fell from the good graces of God and were branded as sinners. Religion teaches us that we need to make our way back to heaven by going to church, confessing our sins and being good people, even though we are really just full of evil and sin.

But once we become aware that we never actually fell from grace, we can awaken back into Perfect Love and Peace. We believed the false voice of the ego (personal false self) that told us we did an evil thing by entertaining the idea of "is there something else besides the Peace of God? Is there a kingdom ruled by something other than the love of God?"

Even though that imaginary nano-second hallucinatory world disappeared in an instant, the ego teaches us that we should feel guilt and shame regardless, and we should fear the punishment that God will inflict. Pretty dumb. But it gets better. The ego says just hide yourself, preoccupy yourself in the memory of a sad, miserable world that never even existed. Anchor yourself in this world by believing you are guilty and projecting your made-up guilt onto "other" dream figures. Then, spend the whole dream complaining, blaming, faulting, protesting and finger pointing. Pretend you are a victim. Pretend you are a victimizer. Pretend you are a hero. Stay deeply preoccupied in the drama. The last thing you want is Peace. Because if you remember Peace, says the ego, then you will remember God. That's how powerful peace is! The ego reminds us not to allow the return of the memory of God, because God will punish you as soon as he gets His hands on you! Be wary of peace. Be suspicious of peace. God won't be far behind. And above all else, for heaven's sake, don't do what Jesus did!

A Course in Miracles Clarification of Terms−5. Jesus−Christ

The name of Jesus is the name of one who was a man but saw the face of Christ in all his brothers and remembered God. So he became identified with Christ, a man no longer, but at one with God.

In *A Course in Miracles*, Jesus tells us that the way to peace is open and that it is inevitable that we will all return to the Peace of Heaven, even though we seem to live in a world full of personal and world problems:

ACIM Chapter 20−IV

You may wonder how you can be at peace when, while you are in time there is so much that must be done before the way to peace is open. Perhaps this seems impossible to you. But ask yourself if it is possible that God would have a Plan for your salvation (peace) that does not work. Once you accept his Plan as the one function that you would fulfill, there will be nothing else the holy Spirit will not arrange for you without your effort. He will go before you making straight your path and leaving in your way no stones to trip on, and no obstacles to bar your way. Nothing you need will be denied you. Not one seeming difficulty will melt away before you reach it. You need take thought for nothing, careless of everything except the only purpose you would fulfill.

Jesus' life as man in the dream was meant to guide us out of the maze of darkness that we have come to know as earth. He did not come to start an organized religion. He had no intention in any way whatsoever to demonstrate suffering and sacrifice. Rather, he lived his life in such a way as to demonstrate to us all that only the Peace of Love is worthy of our efforts.

The only way to remember Love, Jesus tells us in *A Course in Miracles*, is to remove everything that gets in the way of the memory of God as Love. The Introduction to the *Course* starts us off in this way:

This is a course in miracles. It is a required course. Only the time you take it is voluntary. Free will does not mean that you can establish the curriculum. It means only that you can elect what you want to take at a given time. The course does not aim at teaching the meaning of love, for that is beyond what

43

can be taught. It does aim, however, at removing the blocks to the awareness of love's presence, which is your natural inheritance. The opposite of love is fear, but what is all encompassing can have no opposite.

Nothing real can be threatened. Nothing unreal exists.

Therein lies the peace of God.

Only perfect love exists. We are the Perfect Love of God. Nothing can threaten us. Rest here.

Jesus was lost in his love for God.
–Rumi

4

A Tomato Is A Fruit

WE TRAVEL A PATH that seems uncertain and full of doubt. Life for me has been full of ups and downs, peaks and valleys. I have felt supreme happiness and have had my share of pain and anguish. Those words, "pain and anguish," are very much part of my work as a lawyer. Throughout my career as an attorney I have represented people in many areas of the law. Divorce, criminal charges, bankruptcy, social security disability, car accidents and injuries. In all these areas of law, I have essentially dealt with pain, suffering, anguish and heartache. Fear and uncertainty, doubt and struggles fill the courtrooms. Most of my cases involve a trial or hearing during which I explain to the judge or jury my client's pain, suffering, limitation and disability. As I write this, it becomes more apparent that there has been a spiritual reason that this type of law has been my life's work.

This world is a struggle and a challenge for most of us. The world I speak of is the "appearance" world--the false world-appearances that attest to, that witness to, the absence of God. The world that appears to us is a false appearance image of our alleged separation from Heaven's Peace, our Real and Only Home. My experiences in this false world of struggle and pain are representative of our shared experiences. Most importantly, to repeat, that my "salvation," so-to-speak, has been the application of the Truth contained within the pages of *A Course in Miracles.* I have wrapped myself within its pages.

The universal experience of the vast majority of people in this dream world is struggle, pain, doubt, fear, uncertainty, lack, financial scarcity, sickness, misery and ultimately, death. We pretend that we are happy and thriving, when all the while what lurks beneath the surface is fear and anxiety. "Quiet destitution," is what my father called it. There is no question about this. It is undeniable. We see commercial after commercial for anti-depressants and anti-anxiety medications that don't work. The majority of my disability clients, in addition to being in physical pain, also are in mental pain and take antidepressants. After thirty years in the practice of law, not one of them has answered "yes" when I ask if the medication helps.

Spirit, for many years, has encouraged me to write this book, to share this with others. My wife Michelle has encouraged this writing, but I have resisted. Before now, I never felt the time was right. I would always put off writing because I somehow knew, within my heart, that there was something more I needed to learn and understand before sharing my experiences. My aim was to help others become more aware of the Truth I have learned. I have never before felt ready to step out and speak. A Voice deep inside kept gently urging me to "wait, wait, be patient; you have more to learn, more to experience."

But I would think, how frustrating! When will I understand enough to be able to share with the confidence of knowing the Truth, or at least being able to accurately point to the Truth? Along with this frustration was always the equally apparent feeling that I did not want to step out, write and speak until I was sure, until I was confident that I would do no harm with what I said and wrote. The *Prayer of Jabez* has stayed in my mind, reminding me of my intention to do no harm.

I probably have read almost every spiritual book on the planet looking for an answer to the chaos and uncertainty of life. I was seeking Peace. I was seeking to know God, to know the certainty and safety of an all-encompassing Perfect Love that would stay forever, would always know my needs, would always provide, would always be kind and would always know what to do. All of us eventually come to a fork in the road of life wherein we are knocked down so hard, in one way or another, that we are caused to take notice and finally ask, how could a loving God have created this world that I see and experience with my human eyes and bodily senses? If we pay attention, the event or circumstances that precipitates the awareness that something is not quite right with how we thought the world works according to what organized religions have taught, has the potential to skyrocket us out of the orbit of ego spiritual lies.

My search began when I went through a painful, expensive, mind- boggling divorce back in the mid 1990s. I was a successful young lawyer with two small daughters, a nice house, a boat, a dog and a cat. And then, what seemed like all-of-a-sudden, my marriage and life fell apart. Disillusionment and fear set in.

Instead of my plan to stay deeply embedded in the script of the ego, the Plan of Light and Love came to wake me from my belief in the physical world as being real. I became numb and was suddenly immersed in fear and uncertainty. Everything became fuzzy and unpredictable. I wasn't accustomed to living in such uncertainty and chaos.

What I learned later on as I immersed myself deeper and deeper into the Truth within *A Course in Miracles*, was that one of the most effective "tools" of the false self, the ego, is its use of what seems like sudden changes in the flow of what we think of as our life. I would come to learn that these sudden changes don't even have to be catastrophic. They often are what would be considered relatively minor. But the Holy Spirit is ever ready to use these same sudden changes in our lives as an awakening gift:

ACIM Lesson 135 If I defend myself I am attacked

What would you not accept, if you but knew that everything that happens, all events, past, present and to come, are gently planned by One Whose only purpose is your good? Perhaps you have misunderstood His plan, for he would not offer pain to you. But your defenses did not let you see His loving blessing shine in every step you ever took. While you made plans for death, he led you gently to eternal life.

Your present trust in Him is the defense that promises a future undisturbed, without a trace of sorrow, and with joy that constantly increases, as this life becomes a Holy Instant, set in time but heeding only immortality. Let no defense but your present trust direct the future, and this life becomes a meaningful encounter with the truth that only your defenses would conceal.

For instance, the sudden shock can be a minor fender bender accident on the way home from work on a Friday afternoon. Or, the sudden shock can be more serious--like your spouse's unexpected diagnosis of cancer.

In September 2018, my youngest child Kira and I stopped at a small vegetable and flower shop on the way home from her high school. I had passed by this shop many times and had many times resisted the urge to stop in. This Friday afternoon was one of our usual sweltering late summer days here in Florida. We were both thirsty. As we passed the shop, two sandwich boards caught my attention. One said, "Ripe Tomatoes" and other said "Cold Drinks."

I slowed the car and turned into the parking lot behind the shop, and we went in. As we were looking through the coolers to pick out something to drink, my cell phone rang. I could see it was my wife Michelle. I picked it up expecting to hear her happy voice, as it was Friday, finally the end of her work week as a second-grade teaching assistant. Instead, what I heard was her crying. I walked away from my daughter so that she couldn't hear the conversation. My wife had gone to her doctor for a follow up visit after she had had a D&C several weeks before. The follow up was routine, as the doctor expected the biopsy of the small polyp they found prior to the D&C to be normal as it is 99% of the time. Instead, in Michelle's case the biopsy showed a grade 1 endometrial cancer. After a few minutes of talking, she calmed down and said she would be home shortly.

Michelle was referred to one of the top oncologist surgeons at Moffitt Cancer Center at the University of South Florida in Tampa. She had a battery of tests and scans, all of which did not detect any other cancers in her body. After we met the oncologist several weeks later, a radical hysterectomy was needed even though the scans showed no cancer in any other place. Michelle agreed to schedule it as soon as possible.

Our life together as we knew it suddenly was different. Even though I had studied ACIM for 20 years and had been formally teaching it for 3 years, many fear thoughts arose during the weeks between the diagnosis and the surgery. During that time, as much as possible, I called to mind the teachings of the *Course.* In the weeks prior to her diagnosis, I had been directly guided by Jesus and the Holy Spirit to immerse myself in and teach the lessons about Peace, especially #185, I want the peace of God, and #110, I am as God created me. And also, lesson #14 that essentially says that what God did not create, does not exist. I did the best I could to hold the thoughts that God did not create cancer, so it does not exist, and I want the peace of God above all else. Over and over I would roll these lessons through my mind in an effort to bring myself to a state of peace and trust. These lessons were extremely helpful and comforting. I could feel the warm embrace of peace break through the sting of fear thoughts.

Even though Michelle had no interest in studying the *Course*, on a Saturday morning a few weeks before her surgery, I talked to her about wanting the peace of God above all else. We talked about the miracle, or what I call, the Power of Peace. She was receptive, and so the two of us agreed that above all else, we want the peace of God.

Lesson 185 says in part that "*Two minds with one intent become so strong that what they will becomes the Will of God.*"

The evening before we were to meet her surgeon for the first time, for some reason, out of the blue, I was inspired to ask Michelle this question: *Did you know that a tomato is a fruit?* She laughed, being the talented home chef that she is, "Yes of course I know; everybody knows that!" She asked why I had asked that. I said I didn't know.

The next day while we were sitting in the surgeon's office waiting to meet him for the first time, Michelle went down the hall to use the restroom. A few minutes later she came back smiling. "You will never believe what I just saw in the hallway." She then proceeded to tell me that there were large photos of each of the surgeons on the hallway wall. She said each of the surgeons' photos included their personal favorite inspirational quote. She asked me, "Guess what my doctor's quote is?" I said I had no idea.

She then told me that her doctor's photo was of him in a garden, with a vine of ripe tomatoes over his shoulder. Underneath his picture it read:

"Knowledge is knowing that a tomato is a fruit. Wisdom is knowing not to put it in a fruit salad."

I then went down the hall to see for myself. We were stunned. Suddenly, I felt peace and *knew* that Jesus was in charge and had guided us to the right place even within the dream of separation. Ever since Jesus appeared to me in Ft Lauderdale almost 20 years ago, I have done my best to trust his moment to moment guidance. A *Course in Miracles* is my written guide. But his voice and his presence whispers to me throughout the day. I learned a long time ago that I of my own little ego personal self do not have the ability to navigate the dream life on my own. I do my best to step back and let Christ walk ahead of me in all matters. As a lawyer, I step back and let him walk into the courtroom before me. In my personal life, I do the same. The goal isn't to win, rather the goal is for peace for all concerned. It was apparent that the surgeon and outcome had already been gently written into the script of the Holy Spirit. I understood that all that we seem to experience in the dream are past memories of what is no longer in the mind. Years ago, when this became more and more apparent to me for many reasons, I began in earnest asking divinity to show me the truth in a way that I could understand that the dream is actually past and over. I have indeed been shown this in many ways.

And so, it became clear to me that my question the night before about a tomato being a fruit was a memory of mine rising to the surface foreshadowing an event that had already "happened" in the dream of separation that has passed away and was gone.

It also became more apparent to me that what Jesus says in **ACIM, Chapter IV**, is the literal truth that we can trust:

"Once His Plan is the one function that you would fulfill, there will be nothing else that the Holy Spirit will not arrange for you without your effort. He will go before

you making straight your path. Leaving in your way no stones to trip on, no obstacles to bar your way. Nothing you need will be denied you. Not one seeming difficulty but will melt away before you reach it. You need take thought for nothing, careless of everything EXCEPT the only purpose that you would fulfill."

Over the years I have called to mind these words so many times that they have become part of me. I realize now that we all can trust these words to walk ahead of us to dissolve the seeming problem before we arrive. Love, God, has indeed walked ahead of us when we do our best to fulfill our function of forgiveness by looking on devastation and sickness and know, really know, that there is no truth to what we look upon.

And yet fear did its very best to make a run at my resolve to stay in peace. Time after time cancer would call to me telling me how it would ruin our lives. It would snatch my best friend and throw my life into a tailspin. Time after time I chose peace. Fear would find every crack it could find to slip back in. As *Course* student and teacher, I kept thinking I needed to heal my wife's cancer. I needed to be in charge and do something more. I kept asking Jesus what to do. I was frustrated and exhausted from the mental gymnastics. *Trying* to do something began to feel like a heavy burden. I was urged by Spirit to let go and trust and remember that of my own self I could do nothing, but that the Christ that I am in truth does all things that need to be done.

I then became more and more aware that I wanted peace AND I wanted my wife to be healed as well. Jesus impressed upon me to realize that trying to hold both thoughts was NOT peaceful. While the desire of healing seemed to be something I should hold, it actually had a feeling of fear which was anything but peaceful.

Before Michelle's surgery I had gone to bed asking Jesus for a specific answer to a specific question. I wanted to know exactly what single thought he held prior to and during the crucifixion. I wanted to know the thought in which he planted himself so that nothing could pull him from peace. I related to him that ACIM has so many words. I just wanted truth in a simple form. At about 4 a.m. the next morning the Christ in me awoke along with the little me. I could literally feel a previously somewhat dormant part of me, Christ, trying to speak out, trying to break out of a shell. At the same time, I also felt Jesus speaking in unison with the Christ of Paul. The Jesus Christ and the Paul Christ had one voice. There was no difference between the two. The unified voice was that of God's innocent child, His One Creation, His Child, His Love. That Child was the Christ that we all are. And the Christ Child spoke. Jesus, who has taken the lead for us to follow, carries the Christ in all of us. From deep within my heart, in Unison with the Christ in me, Jesus gently whispered, in answer to the question I had asked:

"I know peace".

I could actually feel the vibration of this voice within me. It was as if the real "I" of me spoke. And at the same time, it was Jesus. It was Christ. A long profound silence then followed. I had expected to hear more, that he would give more explanation. So, I asked him again what else he held within during the seeming pain of the crucifixion.

And again, I felt the gentle whisper from within:

"I know peace"

Deep peaceful silence followed. Nothing else followed. I waited. But there was only a peaceful silence. And then I understood the profound Peaceful Silence. The absence of additional words was the exclamation point, the bold print and the underscoring of the fact that there is nothing else to know. There is nothing but the Kingdom of Peace. Christ knows peace and knows nothing else. The Christ in us knows peace and nothing else. Therein is the Power of Peace.

I basked in the silence of the peace of Christ for hours and carried it with me to Moffitt Cancer Center. After Michelle's surgery that lasted well into the evening, I sat with the surgeon. He said all went well, and he found no cancer anywhere at all. At her follow up appointment all biopsies were negative. She needed no additional treatment at all, and the doctor said that he did not expect to see her ever again.

I couldn't resist. I said, as part of our conversation about how cancer changes people's lives, "Doctor, God does not create cancer." He said "No that's not true. God does create cancer. But He also gives us the cure for it". I found his answer very perplexing, but I felt like I had said what the Holy Spirit had guided me to say. It was enough. The doctor heard my words. Perhaps he will recall them in the future when he eventually realizes that God does not create illness. As we left, I thanked him for his kindness and skills. I knew that the light of Christ in the doctor would awaken at the right time. For we are one Christ, one Love. The Power of Peace has walked ahead, clearing the path and removing all thorns.

We can trust a singular thought. Let no other thought come after this thought. Stop here with this thought from Spirit and Jesus Christ, in unison with the Christ we share. Make this thought yours:

"I know peace"

And then feel the warm embrace of peacefulness, of knowing no other thought. Stay here in the Kingdom. All else needed has been provided through no effort of our own. Rest here always. The dream is over. When there is temptation to take in the thoughts of the world, just stop and Know Peace. It is Singular. And then Be Still. Look from peace at the memory of false fear thoughts knocking at the door of the mind. To the fear thoughts and images say, "I don't know you. Be on your way. I know peace. And I know nothing else."

Fear struggles and fights and screams to make itself known. The more emotional shock waves and charge that fear can elicit and inject into the bodily nervous system, the more likely it would win what it perceives as the competition with God to write its meaning (fear) upon the world in place of God's Peace. But we have the power to choose peace instead, as we accept that the world is meaningless.

Lesson 34 I could see peace instead of this.

In this lesson, we are encouraged to be alert to the thoughts that are running through our consciousness. We are encouraged to remember that our task, or "function" here in the dream world of time, is to "forgive" it, to overlook it and instead recognize that it is not-peace, not- love, and therefore not- true and has no existence. So, as we train and discipline ourselves with the desire to feel nothing but the Power of the Peace of God's Love within us, this lesson becomes a torch that we can hold out in front leading us back into the healing, flaming Light of the Truth of our Heavenly state of Perfect Love and Peace.

"I can replace my feelings of depression, anxiety and worry (or my thoughts about this situation, personality or event) with peace."

Even with the seeming seriousness of the news of my wife's diagnosis, the part of me that accepted the world and all its news as meaningless simply asked God to write His Word, instead of the ego's, upon the world that seemed to be happening in my mind.

ACIM Lesson #12 says that if we accept the world as meaningless and allow God's Word to be written upon it, we will be *indescribably happy*! The ego's word/judgment is fear. God's Word is Love and Peace. I asked God to write His Word on the image of Michelle's cancer diagnosis and then did my best to step aside. When the doctors found no additional cancer, we were both *indescribably happy!*

5

Mastery OF LOVE

GOD'S PLAN OF SALVATION for me, as *A Course in
Miracles* calls it, was a far different plan that I, the little
me ego, personal dream self, had. What I really craved
was peace. I just wanted stability and predictability in
my life after divorcing. Some sort of sensible life that
had stability. If something in my mind made sense, it
brought understanding. And when I understood, I was at
peace. Generally, when we don't understand something,
we are not at peace. Rather, not understanding is a
state of uncertainty, instability and upset. I now know
and understand, after applying the Truth of the Course
in Miracles for years, that as Jesus states in the *Course*,
don't bother trying to understand a world that was
imagined, (made) by the false self to *not be*
understandable. I have come to accept that our natural
inclination to love and understand is used by the Dream
of Death (the world that we are imagining or
hallucinating) to hook us into working on the dream

world to make it better and search for love instead of recognizing it as the bad dream that it is and letting it go.

When Michelle was diagnosed with cancer, I had been working with *A Course in Miracles* for 20 years, and I was able to recognize "it", the sudden feeling of a rug being pulled out of my stability. This sudden feeling of instability is the false appearance world doing its best to veil the Peace that is always present. Jesus is quoted in the Bible as telling us that the Kingdom of Heaven is all around us, set out before us, yet we don't see it. *A Course in Miracles* is all about helping us "see" it and feel it as the only Reality. The Power of our Choosing Peace will take us there. For when we make the choice to fall into peace instead of being gripped by fear, all of Heaven responds with the strength of Christ.

The simple, gentle, silent thought of "I choose Peace." dissolves fear. The Power of Peace was gifted to us all by God in our creation. It is the Power that has no opposite, and it belongs to you.

Most of us pretty much move along through life completely occupied by the happenings of what we have all come to accept as normal life. We step on the conveyor belt of birth, education, relationships, children, career, making money, paying bills, getting sick, getting well, marrying, divorcing and then, after all that fun, we get to die. Along the way, most of us are exposed to religion in one form or another. I was deeply exposed to Catholicism. Not many people can escape the feeling that something just doesn't seem right with the explanation of how God "governs "the world. But, at the same time, the vast majority of the world is okay with a thought or two of God on Sundays. It's just easier, we may tell ourselves, to just believe the unbelievable explanations that come forth from traditional religion. Don't question it. Most of the time, the best answer that can be given is that it's all a "mystery." You must have faith in the mystery. What? Faith in a mystery? Faith in a mystery. That never made sense to me. All that meant to me was that the church did not have answer to the most basic questions and preferred to play a game of mystery so that it could seemingly remain as an authority on the who and what of God. Now mind you, I know for absolutely sure that there are many priests, rabbis, ministers and nuns who know Love. My uncle is a priest and he is an example of the living of Christ. But I also know absolutely for sure that the hierarchy of large religious institutions knows very little of the Real Love of God and Jesus. Their seeming authority is grounded in the false teaching of fear, guilt, confession, exclusion, sin and mystery.

The hierarchy of most religions have flat-out distorted Jesus' life and message on earth in order that the church remain in power. The church sustains itself by the claim that it has knowledge that you don't. The church is a concoction of the ego to perpetuate the false concepts of original sin and guilt, which in turn has produced a world full of people filled with shame and remorse. Again, a reminder: the purpose of pointing this out is not to blame. They are doing the best they can with what they were taught. We are all from the same Light and same loving Creator. However, unless we look at it and see it for what it is, we will not shake loose from it and heal.

A Course in Miracles Lesson 127. There is no Love but God's.

No law the world obeys can help you grasp love's meaning. What the world believes was made to hide love's meaning, and to keep it dark and secret. There is not one principle the world upholds but violates the truth of what love is, and what you are as well.

Let me suggest this. How many areas of our lives do we accept an answer of "it's a mystery"? If our child gets a failing grade on an important test, we ask, in an effort to help, what happened? Would our daughter's explanation of "Dad, it's just a mystery" be satisfactory to you? No, of course not.

Imagine you get pulled over by a police officer for doing 45 in a 30-mph zone. You roll down the window and he asks for your driver's license, which you hand over. He then goes back to his car and runs your name and sees you are not a bank robber. He comes back to your car, with the intention of giving you a warning instead of a ticket. But first he asks you, "Why were you going so fast?" You answer, "It's a mystery." The officer is not thrilled with the answer and changes his mind about giving a warning instead of a ticket.

In most, if not all areas of our lives, we are not likely to accept and be satisfied with an answer called "It's a mystery." We don't accept cancer as a mystery. We spend billions of dollars researching for a cure. We don't accept the workings of the solar system as a mystery. We don't stop there at "mystery" and then move no further. What we do is spends millions of dollars and send people into space to chase down the mystery of space.

Jonas Salk wasn't content to accept polio as a mystery. Orville and Wilbur (no offense to anyone named Orville or Wilber, but those are two funny names) Wright didn't accept that controlled flight is a mystery. In 1954, Roger Bannister did not accept the mystery of the "four-minute mile barrier." Good thing he didn't. His "solving the mystery" has since opened the minds of the running world so that at least 1,400 athletes have also broken through what was then a mysterious barrier. Albert Einstein, for all his scientific prowess, wanted only to solve the mystery of God's thoughts.

Why do we, as a whole, remain accepting of the most important "subject" that will ever, ever, present Itself for solving and understanding? Why do we so easily, and rather sheepishly, accept God as a mystery, not capable of being known and understood? Why do we continue to fall prey to the mind-numbing rituals of finding God only in communion bread served in a building we call a church? We go to temples and churches in hopes of finding a real knowing and understanding and a relationship with our Divine Creator. Why don't we push past the canned answers coming out of the churches and the pulpits?

To be sure, many have pushed passed the standard answers. And many continue push to this day. You wouldn't be at all interested in this book if you weren't one of those willing to dare move beyond the explanation that God is a mystery. God is our Creator and Source. We know God, and God knows us.

A Course in Miracles Text Chapter 2

The inappropriate emphasis men have put on beautiful church buildings is a sign of their fear of Atonement and their unwillingness to reach the altar itself. The real beauty of the temple cannot be seen with the physical eye.

The God of Love is not a mystery. Only a god of fear would want to be a mystery. Mystery is not love, because mystery is uncertainty. A god of uncertainty promotes fear and anxiety. When Jesus physically appeared to me in Ft. Lauderdale, Florida in 2000, my life's purpose changed. I was no longer content to accept that Jesus and God were mysteries, to be believed in, but not to be known and understood.

When Jesus appeared to me, he was no longer a mystery to me. The way he would NOT want us to think of him is as a "mystery." He is Real. He is Real because he is pure Love. Love with a capital "L" The Love of God. The Love of God, our Creator.

Jesus whispers to me in this very moment that he wants us to know him as fulfilling his promise, 2000 years ago in the dream, to always be present to help guide us home. That was his promise. "Never," he says, "Think of me a mystery. Never. Please do not accept any teaching that refers to my life, crucifixion and resurrection as a mystery. Do not allow thoughts that belong to organized religion to replace the thoughts that in your heart you know are true. I could never leave you, for you are Love. Remember always that my human life was very much like yours. It was full of joys and sorrows. There were difficulties growing up as a boy and a young man. There was much fun and laughter, and there were many tears and sorrows."

Jesus goes on to say, "I witnessed the difficulties that my parents dealt with day in, day out. It was the story of survival. The gathering of food to feed hungry mouths to keep the body alive. I saw the difficulty of earning money or trading a thing my father made for another thing that may help us survive another day. I witnessed and experienced sickness and pain that could be gone in a few days or may kill with no understanding why. The fear and uncertainty of what the next day would or wouldn't bring constantly haunted the mind."

"I wondered why everything was so uncertain. I wondered why each breath could be my last breath. As the years passed, the world of misery, pain, poverty and limitation began to take its toll on my nature that I felt within. The vast majority of the people in my world, myself included, made extraordinary efforts at love and kindness even in the face of the dire circumstances of the times. This would cause me to wonder why good, loving people had to struggle and strive so much just to make it through the day."

"And then another thought came to mind. What was the point of survival? Why did we struggle so hard and fear so deeply? What was the point of all of this struggle and strife? Why were we engaged with the battle of survival? I saw a conquering army take over the land of my birth. What was the point of the conquering? What did it accomplish?"

"What, I wondered, would happen in the end, if I manage to struggle and strive and conquer the world? What, I wondered, would happen in the end if I mastered the fear of sickness, starvation and poverty? What, I wondered, would happen in the end if I became wealthy and healthy?"

"The question that arose in my mind was this: If I dig in and master, outplay and outwit the fearful challenging world that seems to be my future, what would I achieve? What would happen in the end if I mastered fear? For it became obvious to me that the world appearance was the temptation, the invitation and the challenge to master fear. The invitation was to beat fear, to take it on and fight with it. To bust through its barriers, to accept the challenge. What would I gain in the end? What would be the reward? Peace? Happiness? Love? Joy? I was prompted to consider this over and over again."

"I was urged to look, really look at what I would be fighting and struggling for. The answer was always death. In the end, it was always death that awaited. No matter how many lands were conquered, no matter how many illnesses were survived, no matter how many riches were accumulated, no matter how many children were birthed, no matter how important I could be, in the end death awaited."

"During this time, a voice in my mind became more and more apparent. It was a voice that seemed to speak and yet not always with words. There were urgings and inspirations and inner thoughts. They all had the same theme. They all urged me and pointed me in the direction of Love and Peace. One day, the voice within me asked me, "Yeshua, what if instead of mastering fear, you instead mastered Love? What if you could teach and demonstrate the Mastery of Love? What would await you in the end?"

"The answer came quickly and with certainty. "Love would await you; I promise you. Eternal peace would await you; I promise you. Eternal life would await you, Yeshua; I promise you." The I of Christ had spoken-- the I that is one and the same as the Father."

"These were the Words of God, our Creator and Source. They were the words spoken to me. And they are the words now spoken to you. Accept them as I did. Take them to heart and don't look back. Stay the course with me. Take my hand, my mind and my trust in you, and let us turn from the temptation to master fear and instead accept the invitation to the Mastery of Love. I will show you the way."

ACIM Chapter 2 VII 4

It has already been said that you believe you cannot control fear because you yourself made it, and your belief in it seems to render it out of your control. Yet any attempt to resolve the error through attempting the mastery of fear is useless. In fact, it asserts the power of fear by the very assumption that it need be mastered. **The true resolution rests entirely on mastery through love.** *In the interim, however, the sense of conflict (between love and fear) is inevitable, since you placed yourself in a position where you believe in the power of what (fear) does not exist.*

6

THE LAW OF LOVE

JESUS CONTINUES, "The tears and sorrow that I experienced motivated me to look for another way. My human life, like yours, was a dream of not remembering that my Name and Nature is Love. I eventually came to accept that I was dreaming I had separated from God, from Love. The tears and sorrow and fear prompted me to look for the Truth of Creation, to look for God, our Source. I was not content to accept that God is a mystery."

ACIM Lesson 299

My holiness is far beyond my own ability to understand or know. Yet God, my Father, Who created it, acknowledges my holiness as His. Our Will, together, understands it. And Our Will, together, knows that it is so.
Father, my holiness is not of me. It is not mine to be destroyed by sin. It is not mine to suffer from attack.

Illusions can obscure it, but can not put out its radiance, not dim its light. It stands forever perfect and untouched. In it are all things healed, for they remain as You created them. **And I can know my holiness. For Holiness Itself created me, and I can know my Source because it is Your Will that You be known.**

"I asked within my heart to be shown the truth. I pursued the truth in every moment possible. My days, like yours, were filled with things that needed attending. School. Temple. Work. Yet I was continually urged to master Love. I didn't quite know what that meant yet, but it became a constant thought. I was inspired from within and from teachers who appeared in my life at just the right time and shared just the right words to keep me focused on the mastery of Love."

"There came a pivotal point in my life that solidified my intense desire to master love in the backdrop of so much anger, cruelty and fear in my world. It was a moment of my witnessing the cruel and humiliating treatment of a close friend. I had witnessed much cruel and inhumane behavior in my young life. The time during which I walked the earth, in the dream, was indeed very dark, full of the preoccupation of the struggle to survive. There came a day that broke open my intense desire to understand love and know God. This particular circumstance was nowhere near as severe as much of the misery and horror that I had experienced already. And yet I was touched so deeply that my path to peace and resurrection was solidly, and suddenly, anchored."

"On a sunny, warm afternoon, when I was about 14, I was walking with a friend through the city streets. We were simply enjoying each other's company. She was beautiful, and I was in love. Her eyes were bright, her laughter lifted my spirit, and the touch of her hand felt like a friend from home. Without a warning, a Roman soldier grabbed her around her neck from behind as we were walking. The soldier twisted her around and up off her feet and then pushed her to the ground. The soldier laughed and then went on his way. As I helped her up, I could feel the humiliation in her heart as tears ran down her cheeks. But mostly I could feel the death grip of confusion in her mind. Her confusion as to why cruelty could suddenly arise out of nowhere to shock and shake her out of the previous moment of peace and laughter, was palpable. Her confusion tore at my heart. I could feel her anguish. It was my confusion, too. It was my anguish and fear, too. I so intensely wanted to help her in some way. She looked at me in such a way as if to say, Yeshua, please do something about this. Please make me feel safe and happy again."

"The utter shock and intense fear that we both felt from the sudden change in circumstances rocked my senses. The fear and helplessness that arose produced a rage within my soul. The rage was screaming for an answer. Why? Why the cruelty of this sudden attack upon a peaceful summer afternoon walk? Why did my friend suffer this attack?"

"Even by this stage in my life, I had been exposed to what would be called higher teachings of a spiritual nature that were mixed in with the traditions of the time. I had some familiarity with the notion of how, what I have called the ego in *A Course in Miracles*, works. I understood even at that time, the behavior of most people was driven by fear and control. I was beginning to understand that the world was created by something other than the Love of God. I had been told by sages from other lands and from those in my home that what we saw was imaginary. It was an illusion, they insisted. My young human mind began to subtly accept that this was true. I really did not understand, but a part of me connected with the possibility that the appearance world was a hallucination. I had been told that the world of fear and control thrived on sudden shock, sudden change of circumstances in an effort to illicit a fearful response and to leave us in fearful uncertainty and defensiveness. The appearance world was a constant threat to our well-being. The feeling of being threatened gives rise to having to remain alert to potential harm at every turn. Threat teaches us to become defensive in nature, which, as I came to learn, is the opposite of our nature of peace and openness. Threat is the "brainwashing" or "mind training" of the ego false self-voice. The defensiveness that the ego dream encourages is designed to capture our attention all day so that we don't get a real chance to rest in peace and remember who we are. Instead, we become defensive machines constantly responding to the world or making plans to defend, or to protect ourselves from the world in a continuing effort to find safety in a dangerous place. The sudden intensity of that moment of joy and peace with my friend turned to fear and chaos."

"Shortly after that intense moment, a peaceful, gentle voice whispered to me again:

"Yeshua, you are my son and brother to all whom you see. The promise of Our eternal peaceful life is written upon your heart. Peace is the Power beyond understanding, for in the Knowledge of Peace, there is no need to understand. In the wake of Peace, Love Is. Mastery of Love is yours to teach, through the Power of Our Peace. And so it will be, for it has been done".

"I understood. Somehow, I understood. I did not look back. I began to ask for a way to focus and live in the Kingdom of Peace. I am here now, here in the Kingdom of Peace and Love, as are you. Let me help you remember. You are in the Kingdom where Love would have you be. You just are choosing not to be aware of it. Let me show you the way to open your eyes to the Kingdom's Perfect Peaceful Loving Presence, right here, right now. Let us together remove the blocks and obstacles to your awareness of only Peace. Only Love. And nothing other than Love and Peace. For Love is the Peace that God created you to be. You are Love, and I am with you always."

"Like you, I could not understand that a brother would treat a brother with anything less than kindness and patience. With anything less than an outstretched hand of help. It just did not make sense. A part of me had already accepted the fact that the bodies that the human eye sees are images, pictures that seems to live. I began to have a growing understanding that the escape from the dream world of fear and misery, death and destruction, was the choice for Peace, which needed to be consciously chosen. The passion to share the Love of God was calling. Lack of love and kindness is what drove me to look for and understand the Real God. I knew in my heart that the Truth must be loving and peaceful. And so, I set out to find that God of Love. Lack of love and lack of kindness was my motivator. But it was not my teacher. My Teacher was the Peace of Love."

"I began to accept and talk to Love. Mostly, I joyfully accepted Love's presence and allowed it to talk to me. I gratefully learned to step back from my 'little me' efforts of control, and instead let Love lead the way. As I have said in *A Course in Miracles*:

Text, Chapter 5 II

The principle of Atonement and the separation began at the same time when the ego was made, God placed in the mind the Call to joy. This Call to joy is so strong that the ego always dissolves at Its sound. This is why you must choose one of two voices within you. One you made yourself, and that one is not of God. But the other is given you by God, Who asks you Only listen to it. The Holy Spirit is in you in a very literal sense. His is the Voice that calls you back to where you were before and will be again. It is possible even in this world to hear only that Voice and no other. It takes effort and great willingness to learn. IT IS THE FINAL LESSON I LEARNED, and God's Sons are as equal as learners as they are Sons."

"I eventually came to learn that the Holy Spirit was and is my Right Mind and that all thinking within the Right Mind, the Christ Mind, IS Love Thinking. Love, I came to realize, was much different in all its ways and effects, than what I had previously understood Love to be. You will also come to understand and remember that the Truth of Love is inseparable from Peace. My whole *Course in Miracles* is all about removing the blocks that keep you from remembering Love and Love's Presence. A *Course in Miracles* could just as well have been titled *"The Guide to Remembering Love through Peace."*

A Course in Miracles Chapter 28.I.10

"You need no healing to be healed. In quietness, (peace) see in the miracle a lesson in allowing Cause (God), to have Its Own Effects, and doing nothing to interfere."

"Love became my Teacher because cruelty and fear did not seem to me to be teaching what it was in my nature to learn. Kindness always felt better than cruelty. Peace always felt better than struggle and chaos. Love always felt better than fear. A helping hand always felt better than a pushing away."

"My earthly life became a living example, a demonstration of the Truth of Love. For you see, Love is All there is, was or could possibly be. It took me time to understand, accept and know this. But I assure you. I promise you, that if you follow me and my teaching in *A Course in Miracles*, you too will arrive in the Awareness of Peace and find you are the Love you seek. You will have found and melted into your Source. I will help you come to that realization. I know God, and nothing else. I know peace and nothing else. I know Love. And I know that there is nothing else to know but Love through Peace. You will also, I assure you, come to accept and know only Love, no matter what. Yes, the world of appearances is your imagination of self-inflicted hatred and attack. My *Course in Miracles* will gently lead you to the understanding of the how the ego thought system works and the deception it persists in trying to teach you."

"The appearance world is a dream world in the mind that is past, over and done. It's a threatening, terrifying movie that played in the theater of your mind. It had a short run, so to speak. For you see, on opening night, the night of its debut, Love was the first to enter the theater to preview the fantasy film of death and destruction. Love, the Creator of All That Is, laughed. The ideas in the film were so preposterous and impossible that they were laughable. Ridiculous even."

"Oh, my Goodness," said the God of Love, "I hope the beautiful children of My Light and Love will see this film for what it is and laugh it away as preposterous. But just in case they take it seriously and forget to laugh, I will edit it by placing the spark of the Light of Truth within it and them. I name this spark the Holy Peaceful Spirit. I place this Light of Heaven in each threat, problem and perplexity that seems to occur on the dream screen. This Spirit of Heaven shall be in the same "place" that they will seem to see the problems of trial and tribulation. The place that they will seem to see threats and problems is in what appears to be an outside or external world. But they will come to understand that all problems and threats are in the mind only and so I placed the Holy Spirit, the Answer to every seeming problem, in the mind right next to the illusion of a problem. I place the Light of Love Thinking in each relationship in dream of conflict so that relationships can be used to awaken, rather than to deepen the dream, and can become one of the holiest places on earth, even in the midst of the perception of appearances that seem quite convincing. I place the Light of Love, through the choice for Peace, in each twist and turn of the hallucination so that the choice is always available to awaken at any point of the dream movie of conflict."

"I place the spark of remembrance of the Truth of the Spirit of Holiness as the helper within each of my Children of Love and Light to bring them back to the remembrance of their true Identity as Perfect Love. I

can see that in order to take the movie seriously and
believe that they are actually a character in the dream
of fear, they will have to forget who they are. They will
accept a veil of amnesia, but My Holy Spirit, the Right
Mind of Divine Love, can be chosen to lead them safely
out of the dream by gradually turning the dimmer switch
of unremembered Light back up to Full Bright Radiant
Love. And by placing the Light of Truth within the
dream, all problems and misery in the dream are healed
and solved in the same way. Even though I, Love. the
Loving Creator of All That Is, don't understand the
movie at all and therefore find it completely laughable,
have placed My Love within the Mind of my children's
dream as I see that some may not view the dream of
death as the impossible comic tragedy that it is, and
forget to laugh at it. Some will be enticed or tempted to
only see the tragedy and naturally try to love it or fix it.
They will begin to believe that they are actually "in" the
movie. They will confuse Love with reacting to what
they invented as fear and guilt. The complete amnesia
of identity will make them believe that problem solving
is what they are called to do by love, when actually it
will be the ego's call of false guilt making them believe
they have separated from Love and taken Love's
Throne. The false guilt will result in hiding in this false
dream world of problems and meaninglessness. The
dream appearances will seem to be real to my children
of Light which will cause them to fall deeper and deeper
into the false belief that I, Love, created the world
appearances. They will begin to believe, therefore, that
they need to please Me by being good dream
characters, confessing their sins, and accepting

punishment for not being perfect in an impossible dream of imperfection."

ACIM Chapter 28 I

*The miracle does nothing. All it does is to undo. And thus, it cancels out the interference to what has been done. It does not add but merely takes away. And what it takes away has long since gone but being kept in memory appears to have immediate effects. **This world was over long ago.** The thoughts that made it are no longer in the mind that thought of them and loved them for a little while. The miracle but shows the past is gone, and what has truly gone has no effects. Remembering a cause (the false idea of guilt and separation) can produce illusions of its presence, not effects."*

"I have undone it all by my Love and Laughter," says Love. "My Children sat with me for an instant and it was undone, never to be. But some still watch it, recalling it to their memory attempting to atone for false guilt, not fully accepting that the dream of guilt is healed and past, gone and over. My Holy Spirit remains in their hearts, even in the midst of dreaming that the dream is not over. Only Love and innocence exists. I have placed a Blue Book in the dream. Those Children of My Light who seem to be a bit further along in the dream of awakening back into the Light of Love, shall teach from this Blue Book of Light and Peace. And it shall be called

A Course in Miracles, for it shall awaken the memory of Our Love and Light that We Are."

"The teachers of the Blue Book shall lead the way. They shall walk the Lighted Path of Peace and Love, blazing a trail out of the fog of darkness, into the Bright Light of Heaven. And there shall be one whose name is Yeshua, to later become known as Jesus, the Prince of Peace. He will lead the way. He shall be the first to fully accept my Love within the dream of misery and fear. By doing so, he will remember Me, and he will overcome the illusion of death. His Resurrection shall be the symbol that the dream was never true, that Love can never be torn or separated into pieces and fragments. Yeshua shall teach this to many. This Master Teacher of Love will remain with those who still dream. He shall send his teachers to those who still dream the dream of forgetting that only Perfect Love Exits. All shall eventually return to Heaven by the Realization that only Perfect Love Exists. There is no conflict; it has all been a dream. And it was nothing. My children shall all remember that they are safely Home with Me."

A Course in Miracles Lesson 127 There is no love but God's

There is no love but God's, and all of Love is His. There is no other principle that rules where love is not. Love is a law without an opposite. Its wholeness is the power holding everything as one, the link between the Father and the Son which holds them both forever as the same.

81

*Lord of all pots and pans and things···Make me a
saint by getting meals and washing up the plates.*
–A Pilgrims Prayer, Brother Lawrence

7

BE OF YOUR CHRIST MIND

I REMEMBER VERY CLEARLY early on in my study of
A Course in Miracles being confronted with the
concepts of illusion, appearances and hallucinations.
These terms are very prevalent in the *Course* and are
mentioned over and over again.

They were concepts that were difficult for me to grasp
and believe for what seemed to me to be a very logical
reason. It seemed much too simple of a way to explain
away everything. It's all a dream. It's all a nightmare.
It's all your imagination. You are hallucinating
everything that you seem to see. They are images of
self-attack and vengeance. They don't exist and aren't
there.

Really? It sounded a bit like a cop-out explanation.

So, all I have to do to be happy and at peace is to
accept that what my eyes show me does not exist and

has no meaning. I just need to accept that the sounds my ears hear do not exist. I just need to accept that the sensations that the nervous system my body registers do not exist.

Accepting that the appearance world is a hallucination is key, but it does not come easy for most of us. We are heavily invested in what we see. We have learned, or as the *Course* says, overlearned the ways of the false world:

ACIM Chapter 31 The Final Vision

No one who understands what you have learned , how carefully you learned it, and the pains to which you went to practice and repeat the lessons endlessly, in every form (of fear) you could conceive of them, could ever doubt the power of your learning skill. There is no greater power in the world. The world you see was made by it, and even now depends on nothing else. The lessons that you have taught yourself have become so overlearned and fixed that they rise like heavy curtains to obscure the simple and the obvious. Say not you can not learn them. For your power to learn is strong enough to teach you that your will is not your own, your thoughts do not belong to you, and even you are someone else.

For a long, long time in the story of human history, many different cultures, philosophies and traditions have taught that the world is "Maya," illusion, in one way or another. And yet, here we seem to still be. Here we still are seeing and believing that what we see is true and worth all our effort to participate in and struggle with, to make better and to fix.

As a lawyer now for over 30 years, my job has been to help with legal problems. Someone is disabled or injured, and I help in getting the legal issues resolved. I help make insurance companies pay for things for which they collect premiums and make promises to pay. When people can't return to work because of a medical or severe mental issue, I represent them to get disability approved by social security or an insurance company. I have represented people for bankruptcy to help relieve impossible financial burdens. I represent people in criminal, divorce and child custody proceedings.

 I like being a lawyer. Much of the time it seems that I make a difference by helping relieve a financial or fearful burden. It has always felt to me that I was fixing things or making them right, representing people who have been unfairly treated by insurance companies, corporations, banks and the government.

One day in high school in my sophomore class of social studies, while the teacher had his back to the class, one of the students was talking and generally cutting up. The teacher seemed to ignore it for a bit, but finally turned around, came over to the student he thought was cutting up and really got in his face. The student pleaded innocent. I witnessed the whole thing. And even though I didn't much care for the student he was yelling at, I also knew that he had not done anything. The teacher was accusing an innocent student of being guilty.

At that precise, seemingly ordinary high school moment, I heard a very distinct and clear voice say:

"He is not guilty. He needs a lawyer. You should be a lawyer."

From that moment on, I absolutely knew that I needed to be a lawyer. Before that moment, I was just going to high school. Suddenly, I was going to be a lawyer. I never looked back, and I never second-guessed what I was supposed to do. I was to be a lawyer. Of course, at the time I would not have described it as the Holy Spirit's inspiration, or what I now know as being "Christ led." I know now that I was Christ led and that being a lawyer was part of the plan of Light.

Ultimately, I suppose it doesn't matter the type of work we do, because it is a dream, and we are not really in the world. However, even in the dream, kindness and helpfulness displayed within one's job or profession does in fact help us wake from the dream of fear. So I would say that if you have a calling to work in the "helping" field, and at the same time know that it is a dream, don't ignore that calling. Yes, I know it is dream. Jesus also knew it was a dream. His part in the plan was to demonstrate that only love exists. He clearly showed us that in the face of extreme fear and literal crucifixion, that the Power of Peace and Love could be demonstrated. Many of those in the helping field come face to face with fear and suffering every day and therefore have such a beautiful opportunity to help heal fear. We are to demonstrate in our dream roles as parents, nurses, spouses, teachers, secretaries, doctors, farmers, lawyers and bus drivers, that we are in the Kingdom of Love and Peace. Demonstration of love in chaotic and fearful circumstances is the most potent form of teaching that we can do. It is what Jesus taught and demonstrated.

ACIM Lesson 169 By grace I live. By grace I am released.

Grace is the acceptance of the Love of God within a world of seeming hate and fear. By grace alone the hate and fear are gone, for grace presents a state so opposite to everything the world contains, that those whose minds are lighted by the gift of grace cannot believe the world of fear is real.

Don't let the fact that it is a hallucination or dream cause you to lay back in a lounger and say it doesn't matter what you do. What matters is asking the Holy Spirit where to go, what to do and what to say. We don't have to believe in the world to participate in it. How else can we bring the truth to the attention of the world without seemingly participating in it? I have done lots of jobs before becoming a lawyer. I babysat, mowed lawns, peddled cokes up and down Tampa Stadium stairs, sold beer kegs and washed dishes while in school. None of it was wasted effort. In all of it I could feel the Presence of Peace. It always felt like I wasn't alone. I learned patience, flexibility and satisfaction in something as simple as a freshly cut lawn and in a spotless restaurant kitchen at the end of the night. Is it all a dream? Yes, of course it is. Yet do not let the fact that it is a dream cause you to withdraw. I found peace in mowing lawns and washing dishes and with those I worked with and met along the way. Always make the Peace of God the goal. Standing in the Peace of God in the midst of the chaos of the world is what we are to "do". *If you can find peace while you are in the world, you are no longer of it.*

ACIM lesson 185 I want the peace of God

To say these words is nothing. But to mean these words is everything. If you could just mean them for an instant, there would be no further sorrow possible for you in any form; in any place or time. Heaven would be completely given back to full awareness, memory of God entirely restored, the resurrection of creation fully recognized.

Once we choose Peace, we don't take the world as "seriously" anymore. We see it for what it is. It is a dream world in our mind. Peace will heal the mind, in that our Christ Mind will re-emerge. We each have a part to play which includes being aware that we are pretending to be a figure in the dream who will teach forgiveness by demonstration. Withdraw from the world to the Peace of our Christ Mind and at the same time, participate in the world as a helpful dream character knowing who we *really* are. We are in fact Christ, the Love of God. Be that only while you complete the happy peaceful dream. Be in the world, but not *of* the world.

Lesson 169 By grace I live. By grace I am released.

There is no need to further clarify what no one in the world can understand. When revelation of your oneness comes, it will be known and fully understood. **Now we have work to do, for those in time can speak of things beyond, and listen to words of what is to come has passed already.** *Yet what can these words convey to those who count the hours still, and rise and work and go to sleep by them?*

Suffice it then that you have work to do to play your part. *The ending must remain obscure to you until your part is done. It does not matter. For your part is still what all the rest depends on. As you take the role assigned to you, salvation comes a little nearer each uncertain heart that does not beat as yet in tune with God.*

Where we are experiencing the dream, our "work", our function-- is to forgive or "overlook" appearances because we know that appearances are not God's creation. Yet, at the same time, one does not withdraw. Rather, one stands steadfastly in the Divine Light of Forgiveness in the midst of what appears as suffering and misery. We look steadily to the Light beyond images. Once we accept the purpose of the Holy Spirit in place of the ego specialness whose purpose was to be a substitute for Love, our role in the dream world becomes sacred. We become the hands and feet and eyes and ears of Christ.

If you are a schoolteacher, see in the Light of your Christ Mind, those who appear to be your pupils. If you are a baker of bread, see your customers in the Light of your Christ Mind. If you are a physician, see in Light of your Christ Mind, those that come to you for relief. If you are a parent, see in the Light of your Christ Mind, your child. All and everything is healed within the Light of our Christ Mind.

Each encounter we have in the dream life is another opportunity to wake to the holiness of our Christ Mind. See, feel and know your Christ Mind. Extend your Christ Mind to all those you see. They can only be in your Christ Mind. There is nothing outside our Christ Mind. The Power of Peace is our Christ Mind.

A Course in Miracles, Text Chapter 18 IV

There is nothing outside you. This is what you must ultimately learn, for it is the realization that the Kingdom of Heaven is restored to you. For God created only this, and he did not depart from it nor leave it separate from Himself. The kingdom of heaven is the dwelling place of the Son of God (the Real Holy You), who left not his Father and dwells not apart from Him. Heaven is not a place nor a condition. It is merely an awareness of perfect Oneness, and the knowledge that there is nothing else; nothing outside this Oneness and nothing else within.

Operate on your patients, represent your clients, teach the children, clean out the clogged toilets, mow the lawns, bake the bread, chop the wood and wash the dishes. And as you do so, be aware only of the Holiness of your Blessed Christ Mind. The Kingdom of Heaven is spread out before us. See it and share it right where you are in the dream. How is this shared? Trust that you are the Christ, the Love and Light of God, all that He Created. In that trust, the Love that is Christ can't help but be shared. Trust this Fact.

*Death is the central dream from which
all illusions stem.*
  –ACIM Manual For Teachers 27

8

THE MIRACLE LAUGH AT DEATH

UNTIL APRIL 2016, I did not feel ready to speak about
or teach *A Course in Miracles*. As the years went on,
despite studying and applying the Course every day as
consistently as possible, there was a feeling inside that
I just wasn't ready to speak publicly yet. Jesus kept a
gentle whisper in my heart that said, "Not yet; be
patient, just a bit longer." On one hand, this gave me a
certain level of contentment that I was on the right path.
On the other hand, I was a bit frustrated not knowing
what I was waiting for to happen that would give me the
green light. Even with this frustration, I had a recurring
request of my heart that asked the Holy Spirit to make
sure not to allow me to publicly speak and teach until
such time as I could do no harm or mislead anyone with
my words. This is the *Prayer of Jabez.* I wanted to be
sure that the message I would deliver would be as pure
as possible.

"Oh, that You would bless me indeed, and enlarge my territory, that Your Hand would be with me, and that You would keep me from evil, that I may not cause pain".

The defining moment that I felt safely granted me permission to teach without harm, was the Miracle that happened in April 2016 in the home of my parents, Peter and Mary Cardillo. This Miracle was the experience and the understanding that Jesus kept telling me would come. It was the inner release in me of what I had come to understand as the divinity of my Christ Mind, the Christ Mind that we all have, share and are. It has allowed me to know and to go forward in confidence. The experience of this Miracle taught me that I could step back in Trust, knowing for certain, that God has a Plan for our Salvation, for our Peace, and for our return to the state of Heaven.

Here is what happened in April 2016 in my father's living room. This is the Miracle that convinced me that is was time to publicly write and speak, inspired by Jesus and the Holy Spirit.

My father Peter had retired early from the water treatment company that he owned in Baton Rouge Louisiana. He and my mother moved back to Tampa after 20 years or so of living in Baton Rouge. They had previously lived in Tampa, but when I was about to start college at the University of South Florida, my father took a job in Baton Rouge that would ultimately lead to him owning his own company with two partners in the commercial water treatment business. His retirement was really not planned as his two partners forced him out early at age 59, a seemingly unfair circumstance. Yet, my father, who never failed to look for the good in everyone, came out on the other side in peace and in knowing that God was with him in all things. The forced early retirement turned out to be a blessing, which I know for certain did not surprise my father.

In his retirement, my mother kept him busy building and remodeling the old house they bought. He was a remarkable self-taught carpenter, electrician and painter. As a kid, I worked on many home projects by his side and to this day, whenever I work on something at home or as a lawyer, I hear his words, "If it's worth doing, it's worth doing right." As the years went on, he enjoyed his 17 grandchildren, golf, his home projects, spending time with my mother, going to church and travel. Because my parents lived a block from Old Tampa Bay, my father would take early morning walks along the bay on the sidewalk that runs along its edge.

While on his walk one day, he was accidentally knocked over by a bicyclist. He fell to the ground, hit his head and was unconscious for a brief time. After an overnight in the hospital, he was released, having been diagnosed with a concussion and an expected full recovery. Unfortunately, as time passed, it became apparent that he had suffered some brain damage that began to mimic dementia or Alzheimer's. As his ability to communicate with words began to fade slowly, over a period of about

3 or 4 years, he became more confused and fading in his ability to understand the world around him. And yet, he always smiled and had light in his eyes, and love in his heart.

It began to become apparent that he knew he would soon make his transition into spirit. He had begun saying he was going to die, as he grew weaker from not eating much and just losing his desire to live. He remained happy, yet it became clear that the end of his struggle to live was near.

Just a few months prior to this time, I was drawn to the passages in the *Course in Miracles* that spoke about the illusion of death. There are many such passages in light of the fact that the *Course* is centered around getting us to understand that the world we seem to live in is a world of death and destruction and misery. It's a dream of death that was NOT created by the God of Love that created us perfectly as spirit.

There came a point when my mother thought that the time was right for my father to receive what Catholics call the sacrament of Last Rights. Essentially, this is when a priest gives Communion, blesses with holy water, and says prayers for the person who may be dying.

On the morning that the priest was to be at my parents' house to administer the Last Rites, I was led very specifically by Jesus to the following passage:

A Course in Miracles Text, Chapter 19 IV C;

And so it is with death. Made by the ego, it's dark shadow falls across all living things, because the ego is the enemy of life.
*And yet a shadow cannot kill. What is a shadow to the living? They but walk past it and it is gone. But what of those whose dedication is not to live; the black draped "sinners", the egos mournful chorus, plodding so heavily away from life, dragging their chains and marching in the slow procession that honors their grim master, lord of death. **Touch any one of them with the gentle hands of forgiveness**, and watch the chains fall away, along with yours. See him throw aside the black robe he was wearing to his funeral and **hear him laugh at death**.*

Although I had read this passage many times before, it had obvious significant meaning to me that morning. I was clearly led to this passage. I had simply opened ACIM randomly to that particular page. Death was the topic, and Jesus was telling me about laughing at death, "To touch it with the gentle hands of forgiveness." Was I supposed to literally laugh at death by "forgiving" it? Should I believe Jesus? A long time ago, I decided that I either believe him 100%, or not at all.

Yes, I decided to gently laugh at the idea of death with Jesus, by "touching it with the gentle hands of forgiveness." I innately understood that the silent inner laughter at death also included forgiveness, because forgiveness is the "overlooking" of the appearance world of death. Laughter, silent sweet gentle inner laughter, *is forgiveness* of the appearance world of death in all its many forms. About two hours after reading in *A Course in Miracles* that I was to gently laugh at death by touching it with the hands of forgiveness, I attended the Last Rites ritual at my parents' home.

My dad was sitting in his favorite chair, very lucid and really not at all appearing as if he needed last rights. He did not look sickly. He smiled at the priest who quickly began the sacramental rites. The priest brought out holy water and walked over to my father, who was wearing his New Jersey Shore baseball cap and a smile. As the priest approached to sprinkle holy water, my father tipped and then removed his hat, and smiled.

As the water hit my father, he began to laugh. I couldn't believe it; he actually began to laugh! Here we were at this solemn ceremony of death, and my dad was laughing at death! The priest looked completely confused. All I could do was laugh inside right along with my father. Oh my gosh I thought, Jesus wasn't kidding about our need to laugh at death by forgiving it. I could not stop smiling. The gentle laughter was the forgiveness. The laughter was not taking death seriously, knowing it was ours to overlook. As I held the awareness that there is no death, I "forgave" it. In that forgiveness, I witnessed the Miracle of the overcoming of death.

ACIM Text Chapter 19 IV i

*What better way to teach the first and fundamental
principle in a course on miracles than by showing you
the one that seems to be the hardest can be
accomplished first? The body but can serve your
purpose. As you look on it so will it seem to be. Death,
were it true, would be the final and complete disruption
of communication (with God), which is the ego's goal.*

In the *Course* Jesus tells us that the false world began
when we forgot to laugh at the idea of being able to
separate from God, Eternal Life. He says we
"Remembered NOT to laugh" at the idea of death. And
so, when we took the idea of a world of death seriously,
we began to believe it and became lost in the dream of
death.

ACIM Text Chapter 27 VIII

*Let us return the dream (of guilt/death) he gave away
unto the dreamer (us/me), who perceives the dream (of
guilt/death) as separate from himself and done to him.
Into eternity, where all is one, there crept a tiny mad
idea, at which the Son of God remembered not to laugh.
In his forgetting did the thought become a serious idea,
possible of* **both** *accomplishment and real effects.
Together we can laugh them both away and understand
that time cannot intrude upon eternity. It is a joke to
think that time can come to circumvent eternity, which
means there is no time.*

I had just been shown the healing miracle effect of my laughing at the thought of death. Not just the physical death of the body, but of all forms of death, all thoughts that are not happy. Remember, Jesus defines death as the one idea that underlies all feelings that are not supremely happy.

ACIM Lesson 167 There is one life and that I share with God.

*In this world there appears to be a state that is life's opposite. You call it death. Yet we have learned that the idea of death takes many forms. It is the one idea that underlies all **feelings that are not supremely happy**. It is the alarm to which you give response of any kind that is not perfect joy. All sorrow, loss, anxiety, and suffering and pain, even a little sigh of weariness, a slight discomfort or the merest frown, acknowledge death. And thus deny you live.*

This passage from Lesson 167 is among the most important in the *Course*. Slowly read it over and over again. Let it sink in. Here, Jesus is encouraging us to pay attention to our thoughts. He wants us to be aware of the thoughts and feelings we have. As we go through our day, we need to be aware of our belief in death by catching ourselves in "even a little sigh of weariness." I remember when I began to become aware of these thoughts and feelings. We are so accustomed to accepting that weariness is just part of life. But now we see that the seemingly innocent sigh of weariness is really a guilt sigh of the belief in death.

An antidote, so to speak, for when we catch ourselves in a sigh of death or response of any kind that is not joy, quickly realign with Heaven, by simply saying within our hearts, "I choose the Peace of God." Then trust that this choice is honored and granted immediately by the Holy Spirit. The Power of Choosing Peace is power because it is always granted. As Jesus tells us in the Course, Cause is never separate from Effect. Cause, with a capital 'C', *is* its Own Effect. Therein lies the Power of Peace. Peace of God is Cause. It is One and indivisible.

It is my hope that *A Course in Miracles* grabs you and it doesn't let you go. That's my prayer for you. We are all one, and we all share only one need. That need is to return to Heaven by removing the obstacles (lies) that stand in the way of our remembering the truth of who we are, which is pure perfect, innocent Love. *A Course in Miracles* is dedicated to that purpose. Read it and put it into practice in your life. What would Jesus say? He'd say, read it and practice it.

The body's death to me now is like going to sleep.
No fear of drowning. I'm in another water.
–Rumi

9

OVERCOMING DEATH

THOSE WHO HAVE STUDIED *A Course in Miracles*, know that in many places, it says death is but an illusion. My experience with my father was a demonstration of that truth. Yet, I felt there was more to understand and appreciate. The acceptance of the laughability of death was still a bit mind boggling. Clearly though, I was being led to something deeper. I became thirsty to remember and know the Truth. I kept asking to be shown Truth.

I asked Jesus for more understanding of the concept of "death." I intuitively knew that it was important to grasp the knowing that death was not real. I kept asking Jesus to show me somehow or give me the understanding of "how" he overcame death. He says in many places in *The Course* that when he overcame death, we all overcame death. But I didn't feel that way at all. Intellectually, I understood that death is a false concept.

Death is a false idea that was made up and accepted as real. Now I found myself in the circumstance with my father in the dream of death.

When thoughts of writing this book began to come to me years ago, there was a knowing that the key to understanding *The Course* and truly helping others to understand was the *demonstration* of the Truth contained within its pages. The purpose of this book is to share with you how I have applied the Truth found in *A Course in Miracles* to the events and situations that have arisen in my earthly life. For me, this has been the journey. The studying and then ultimately the application of the *Course* principles and lessons to what confronts me in my daily life. That's the classroom. The earthly life. What arises. Apply the lessons and principles to what arises. Then Trust in Jesus and the Holy Spirit that what they teach is true. Jesus tells us that only the Truth is True and nothing else is true:

ACIM lesson 152 The power of decision is my own.

*No one can suffer loss unless it be his own decision. No one suffers pain except his choice elects this state for him. No one can grieve nor fear nor think him sick unless these are the outcomes that he wants. **And no one dies without his own consent.** Nothing occurs but represents your wish, and nothing is omitted that you choose. Here is your world, complete in all its details. Here is its whole reality for you. And it is only here salvation is.*

You may believe that this position is too extreme, and too inclusive to be true. Yet can truth have exception? If you have the gift of everything, can loss be real? Can pain be a part of peace, or grief of joy? Can fear and sickness enter in a mind where love and perfect Holiness abide? Truth must be all inclusive, if it be truth at all. Accept no opposites and no exceptions, for to do so is to contradict the truth entirely.

Salvation is the recognition that the truth is true, and that nothing else is true.

As God created you, you must remain unchangeable, with transitory states by definition false.
***And that includes** all shifts in feeling, alterations in conditions of the body and the mind; in all awareness and in all response. This is the all-inclusiveness which sets the truth apart from falsehood, and the false kept separate from the truth, as what it is.*

My yearning to understand the falsity of the concept of death also led me to a book written by Nook Sanchez titled *"The End of Death."* I highly suggest this book to anyone who wants help in gaining a deeper clarification and understanding of the lie of death and how it appears in our life in many forms that we would never guess are actually forms of the concepts of death. Nouk does an amazing job of taking one through the various passages in *The Course* to help explain and understand the concept of death.

For me, one of the key lessons in **ACIM** is **Lesson 58,** which is a condensed version of **Lessons 36-40.** Understanding and accepting my Holiness in place of-- or instead of--guilt/death, was a "get off the fence" acceptance for me. It felt like a line drawn in the sand, a definite clear decision I was to make. Either I am the Holiness as I was created by God, or I am the presence of death, as made up and imagined by the ego/personal self. It was a feeling that I needed to pick a horse and ride it. I felt I could no longer try to ride both the dark horse of death and the white horse of Love. It was time to pick my horse, pick my lane and ride it to the finish line.

At this time of grappling with the understanding of the falsity of the concept of death, I had also finally become weary and tired of the miseries of everyday ups and downs, financial lacks and challenges. I was inspired to go even deeper into surrender and let go. It was time to make a final choice and then steadfastly trust. I could no longer struggle with trying to make the things of life work. For no apparent reason my business dropped off several years prior. I was successful in my cases, but the number of cases declined for no discernable reason. This led to our home being foreclosed, credit card debt and the transfer of my office building back to the bank. I lost all the equity in my home and office that I had built over the years. Everything I did to increase business seemed to fizzle for very bizarre reasons. Cases that I had worked on for years that had the potential for significant financial reward fell flat. Nothing was making sense anymore. On one particular case, I brought in a highly regarded law firm to push the case over the finish line, only to see it fizzle out to nothing after years of work and significant investment of money. After a good while, I began to realize that perhaps room was being made in my life for something in addition to the practice of law. I was, in fact, being shown the truth as I had asked. Yet it was confusing and frightening. Spirit urged me to continue to practice law, but to also focus more and more on *A Course in Miracles.* I was told I would have what was needed to accomplish what I was here to do.

It was against this backdrop that my father appeared to be approaching his physical death. By this time, the understanding of the fact that there is no death had jelled within me. It just jelled. That's the best way that I can describe it. The feeling became real; much more than a belief. It became a very peaceful knowing. I had accepted and trusted that Jesus is telling us the Truth in ACIM. The alternative is to believe that he is telling us lies. I chose to believe that there was no way Jesus was giving misleading instruction. I had seen proof in my life too many times. I surrendered to the Truth that he teaches as deeply as I could.

One day not too long after the Last Rites ritual, I sat with my father as he grew more tired. The injury to his brain had taken its toll. On one hand, I was humanly saddened by my father's plight. He was, and remains, the demonstration to me of love in my life. To see him lose his ability to communicate and participate in life was unbearable for me. Yet, on the other hand, I knew that he was Spirit, and I was called by God to help him remember that he was the Holy Christ, the perfect Son of God.

I was led to sit with him in silence. I would simply hold the Truth within as I sat with him. Silently I would repeat over and over "Dad, our Holiness is our Salvation, there is no death". Over and over I would repeat this as I sat with him. Yet nothing seemed to change. He looked at me and tried to smile. But he wanted to go to bed. He was tired. He was done. My mother helped him to bed as he kept repeating that he was dying. He was frustrated and in a bit of pain from not eating. He closed his eyes, and it was apparent that he would pass very soon. I said my goodbyes and thanked him for being my father. My brother Luke, who was also there, agreed that he would be passing soon, probably within a few hours.

That night I kept expecting a call from my mother, but it never came. Instead, the next day when I called to check on him, my mother said that my sister Mary Jane had taken him to the beach and for ice cream at John's Pass in Clearwater, about 20 miles across the bay. What? How could he be strong enough to even get out of bed? After he came home later that day, my sister reported that he had a great time walking around the shops and eating ice cream.

This didn't make sense. He clearly was at the end when I left him. Something within him had changed. Jesus clearly impressed upon me that what changed was that my belief in death had been overcome by the acceptance of Truth of our Holiness. Then, because we are One and there are no separate minds, when I silently shared this thought with my father's Christ Mind, he accepted his Holiness. My Christ Mind and his Christ Mind joined in the recognition of our Innocent Holiness.

As **Lesson 38** says:

"There is nothing my holiness cannot do."

Your holiness reverses all the laws of the world. It is beyond every restriction of time and space, distance and limits of any kind. Your holiness is totally unlimited in its power because it establishes you as a Son of God, at one with the Mind of his Creator.
Through your holiness, the power of God is made manifest. Through your holiness the power of God is made available. And there is nothing the power of God can not do. Your holiness then can remove all pain, end all sorrow, and solve all problems. It can do so in connection with yourself and with anyone else. It is equal in its power to help anyone because it is equal in its power to help anyone because it is equal in its power to save anyone.

Our Holiness, our Identity, the Truth of our Creation, is the "what" of what we share. It is our common bond. Our Holiness is the Love of our Creator. It is the sweet nectar that holds us as one. It is our innocence, our Divine essence. Holiness is our Christ Mind, our Love. Within Our Holiness, is the Power of Peace. Our holiness *is* the Peace of God.

As I accepted the truth of my Holiness, I began to feel whole, more complete and more at 'home.' And because we all share that same Home (Christ Mind), the recognition of that feeling is really the shared feeling within, where there are no gaps of "not love" or "not Holiness." As this feeling deepened within me, I trusted that I could share this with my father without saying a word. I realized that my father's body was an image in our Christ Mind.

A few days or so after he made what appeared to be the "ice cream recovery," my father, Peter, began growing weaker again and talked about dying. So, I sat with him again, silently holding to the Truth, that Holiness is our Salvation. That the Peace of Holiness and Love is the only power that there is. That there is no death. That our Holiness is our salvation because it is who and what we are. Holiness is our Identity. And in Holiness there is no death. We made up all other identities of who we are. I carried these thoughts gently, but with faith, within my divine mind as I sat with my father. I felt a sense of peace of eternity. I felt the Truth of the fact that there is no death. The Life of God is eternal Life, and I have no other Life than that of God's Life. There is no death of Life.

Within a few minutes of holding to the Truth, my father, who was sitting with his eyes closed by the fireplace in his green leather easy chair, suddenly opened his eyes and smiled. He became very alert and excited. And he began to speak.

He said "I am not Peter! I am not Pete!" Then he began excitedly tugging on the leg of his pants, smiling and repeating, "this (body) is not me··· this is not me!" He then closed his eyes peacefully to rest again.

In that moment I did not realize what had just happened. It was a few hours afterwards that I began to understand the significance of what had occurred. In the dream of time, we forget our true identity as Holiness, as Spirit. We make a false identity in the dream of the forgetting of our union, our oneness with God. We have complete amnesia here in this world. Because we chose to forget the constant, eternal Presence and Love of God, we wander within our minds, in a dream of the absence of God. The dream we hallucinate is a dream of the unawareness of God's never ending, all encompassing, all pervading, all providing Perfect Love. Jesus tells us in *The Course* that we are much too tolerant of allowing our minds to wander from being aware of Perfect Love.

ACIM Chapter 2 IV

*You are much too tolerant of **mind wandering** and are passively condoning your mind's miscreations.*

And:

ACIM Lesson 96 Salvation comes from my one Self

Salvation comes from my one Self. Its Thoughts are mine to use.
*Then seek its Thoughts and claim them as your own. These are your real thoughts you have denied, and let your **mind go wandering** in a world of dreams, to find illusions in their place.*

A Course in Miracles is a book of our Holy Remembrance. It is a book 'dictated' by Jesus through Helen Schucman. It is in fact, the Word of God. It is the call to remember who we really are, the call to stop pretending that we are not Love and not Innocent and not at Peace. It is the map to retracing our steps, to retracing the false thought process that has led us deep into this world of misery, pain, sickness, fear, scarcity and death.

As this remembering of Truth becomes more and more clear, it is automatically shared with those around us, and in fact, with all of the "world." In my remembrance of the Truth, my father woke up, or remembered who he is. *"I am not Pete ⋯. this (body) is not me!"*

One of the core principles that Jesus calls on us to remember throughout his teaching in *A Course in Miracles* is that "I am not a body, I am free, I am as God created me."

My father's waking up to the Truth of who he is, to recalling or remembering of his real Name, the Holiness of Love, was such a gift to his own journey Home and to mine. You see, because he was able to mirror the sense of Holiness that I had come to accept as my essence, as mySelf, I was gifted with the witness to the Truth of who and what I Am. As I remembered, my father remembered. And having excitedly accepted, he remembered his Self again. The seeming power of death was overcome. Death is a false concept related only to the false personal identity that we pretend we are in this dream world. Death wanted to obliterate the Christ within my father. But it could only do so if I believed we are anything but Eternal Life, Eternal Holiness and Love. In this world, my father was full of love. It was his nature even in this false world. His nature, or "name," has always been love, patience and kindness. But in the overlay of the forgetting of our inseparability from God, we come to believe that we are sinners and imperfect. Because of that false belief, we hide and wander in what we think of as a world in which we have the opportunity to prove we are "good" and can behave, thereby pleasing an angry and judgmental God. We believe, as we are taught by most organized religions, that if we please God enough, if he judges us as worthy and sorrowful, we just might be allowed into Heaven. The world's religions teach us that we must first accept ourselves as unworthy and as sinners. We must accept that we are flawed. We are even instructed to believe that there was a man named Adam and a woman named Eve and because they ate an apple from a tree that God said not to eat from, we, in our seemingly present day world, are also sinners and not worthy of God's Perfect Love and Acceptance. Somehow, thousands of generations later, you and I and my father are sinners. There is no blame in pointing this out, for we made it all up and agreed to take is seriously.

Seriously?

The concept of death was overcome by Jesus. He overcame the concept of death for us. In *A Course in Miracles,* Jesus asks us to accept the fact that he overcame it and that we share in that overcoming. All of "us," as the Divine Christ Mind created by God, are joined. As minds, we are not separate, although the dream world of ego, which we made, does its very best to convince us that there is you and there is me in separation from each other. Jesus taught us that the false world appearances are designed by the false thought system of the ego to "think apart" from God and each other.

Our time in the dream is spent attending to what seems to be problems of health, finances and most of all, relationships. Our minds are taken up and preoccupied with fixing problems within the illusionary dreamworld where God isn't. We all have different problems, different particular wants and needs. All of these problems, wants and needs clash and bang into each other. Conflict and struggle mark our days. Chaos and insanity rule the world we see. We must, as Jesus teaches, decide to see differently. And in order to see

differently, we must look from the point of view of the
Truth. We must see from the point of view of Peace. We
are as God created us, and from that point of view, all
things work together for good, even in the dream. For
once we accept the purpose of Light, we enter the
Happy Dream of Awakening, gently dreamed for us by
Christ.

ACIM Text Chapter 4 V. 1

*All things work together for good. There are no
exceptions except in the ego's judgment (eyes of the
ego/personal mind).*

We must look with the forgiving, gentle, peaceful Eyes
of God upon the false world we accepted as our reality.
We don't blame others. We accept that we have done
this to ourselves and that the dream characters are
playing the parts we assigned to them in our own little
world. We can accept that we remain as we were
created. We can naturally "look" with these eyes. We
must look out from the knowing that we can see from
the Holiness of our Christ Mind. And the only "thing"
there is, the only "thing" that exists is the Presence of
Perfect Love. Nothing else is true, because nothing else
exists. We rest, rest, rest in the Loving Presence of
Holy Innocence where the thought of death cannot
enter. We are only truly alive when we know Perfect
Love. Warm smiling thoughts are our real thoughts we
think with God. Death thoughts are thought by the ego

mind which tries to convince us that they are our thoughts. But we are Christ, and in that Real Identity, we cannot have a death thought. Again:

ACIM Lesson 167

Yet we have learned that the idea of death takes many forms. It is the one idea that underlies all feelings that are not supremely happy. It is the alarm to which you give response of any kind that is not perfect joy. All sorrow, loss, anxiety and suffering and pain, even a little sigh of weariness, a slight discomfort or the merest frown, acknowledge death. And thus, deny you live.

Death is the thought that you are separate from your Creator. It is the belief that conditions change, emotions alternate because of causes you cannot control, you did not make, and you can never change.

When my father opened his eyes and smiled, he smiled because he remembered God. And in doing so, he remembered his own Identity that we have all forgotten. Jesus remembered it for us in the resurrection. As best as I could, I trusted that Jesus had overcome the concept of death for us. In that trust that I shared with my father, he too was resurrected back into the Light of Truth. Light prevailed as Jesus promised. Light prevailed in the face of the threat of the darkness of death. Light, being the Power of God in which we abide, can and does shine away all false ideas and thoughts. Light, Love, Truth, and Peace shined into the mind of

113

my father from Jesus and "me," and overcame the thought of death. Jesus is in fact our savior, but not in the way that the world would have us believe.

This Miracle of my father's transition back into the Light of Love was "the proof of the Truth." that what Jesus teaches us in *A Course in Miracles* is the Truth. The lessons he teaches are True. Moreover, the practicality of his words and their application to our daily lives works. By that I mean that we will see and feel the results of accepting and "applying" the Truth of his words.

ACIM Lesson 38. There is nothing my holiness cannot do.

Through your holiness the power of God is made manifest. Through your holiness the power of God is made available. And there is nothing the power of God can not do. Your holiness then, can remove all pain, can end all sorrow, and can solve all problems. It can do so in connection with yourself and with anyone else. It is equal in its power to help anyone because it is equal in its power to save anyone.

And also:

ACIM Lesson 39. Our Holiness is our salvation.

Your holiness is the answer to every question that was ever asked, is being asked now, or will be asked in the future. Your holiness means the end of guilt, and therefore the end of hell. Your holiness is the salvation of the world (that you see in your mind), and your own. How could you, to whom your holiness belongs be excluded from it? God does not know unholiness. Can it be that he does not know His Son?

Thank You, Angels. Thank You, God.
-Gary Spivey

10

RADIO SPIRIT

I BEGAN STUDYING and practicing *A Course in Miracles* during my divorce over 20 years ago. It was at that time I met a man who profoundly changed my view of life.

I was leaving downtown Tampa after a court appearance. I got in my car and turned on the radio to a local FM music radio, the Ron and Ron show. There was a guest psychic on the show. Between songs he would take phone calls from people who had questions. His name was Gary Spivey. After listening to a few of the questions and his answers, I was thoroughly impressed with the accuracy of his answers and the compassion in his voice. I didn't know it at the time, but there was a part of me that recognized his Spirit even though I had never met him. At that time in my life, my exposure to spirituality consisted of growing up in the Catholic Church, being educated (and occasionally smacked) by nuns in black outfits and going to church every Sunday.

Back then, the Catholic Church taught me that anyone who wasn't Catholic was pretty much headed to hell. Even worse, even though I was Catholic, I was headed there too, unless I acknowledged and confessed my sins. I was also never, ever to even entertain the thought of questioning the teachings of the church, because God was always watching me and would know what I was thinking. I realize that the Catholic Church has evolved a bit since then, but that was my experience and the experience of much of the world.

With this fear-filled background from the church, I certainly had no inclination to talk to a psychic or even consider anything a psychic may have to say, especially ones that were on a morning radio show! In spite of that, there was something about Gary Spivey, something that I would come to know as the love of God in his voice.

Within a day or so of hearing him on the radio, I was stopped at a red light after attending another court hearing. I was in a state of confusion, fear and pain about my life situation. Everything was upside down. I was trying to hold everything together but felt like my life was falling apart at every turn. My marriage was falling apart, and I was running on empty.

So, sitting at that traffic light in downtown Tampa that morning, I pretty much was at the end of my ability to find some peace in my life. There was so much upheaval. I had the radio on to the same station, and I again heard the psychic answering questions. It was in that moment of surrender to that helpless feeling that I felt an inner prompting to pick up my cell phone and call the radio show. The "prompting" actually felt like an inner light that smiled. That's the best way I can describe it. I pulled over into a parking lot and dialed the number. I really did not expect to get through, because this psychic had become so popular that the call-in phone lines were jammed with people wanting to speak with him.

As I would realize later, Divinity arranged it so that my call got through to Gary. I was stunned when I heard his voice. Before I called, I wasn't even sure what I wanted to ask him. I felt like I really just wanted to ask him some law business related questions, which is what I did. I didn't ask anything about my personal life. He answered my questions patiently and with amazing clarity. Our conversation only lasted a couple of minutes, and we were done. Or so I thought. Just as we finished, he asked if there was anything else I would like to ask. I said no. He said, "Well, I have more to tell you. God is telling me to have you call me off the air so that we can talk." I was intrigued and so I numbly agreed. We went off air during a commercial and he gave me his personal phone number. He emphasized it was important to call him. I said I would. I had no idea of what God wanted me to know, or that God would have an interest in my life. While I was hopeful, I really wasn't convinced that this psychic could be of help to me.

When I called him later that day, he reiterated that "God" had more to say to me, that there was more for me to know. This was so different from what I expected. Again, I didn't know that God cared. The God I was taught about was very judgmental and punishing. Everything was about sin. Venial sins and mortal sins. Impure thoughts and impulses. A God that gets angry and impatient with his unworthy children. So angry he floods them out sometimes. Or sends locusts and snakes to terrorize them. He even had what's called the "Angel of Death" pay a visit to his children to shake them up. And at one momentous point in history, this God sent his "only son" to earth to be our savior. We are taught that the plan of this angry God is that his son Jesus would be spit upon, tortured mercilessly and nailed to a wooden cross. Then his son would spill his blood and sacrifice his body so that all the worthless sinners of the time and for all time to come would somehow be a saved sinner. They would be saved by his blood. If you drink his blood and then eat bread that we are told is miraculously really the flesh of his body, we may be able to get to heaven. But wait. There's more. You have to confess your sins to a man in a black outfit who is supposedly Jesus's representative on earth.

I now understand this is a false power being claimed by a human institution. Most people are coming to this realization. Again, no blame is intended. But what is false is false.

So, this feeling of God wanting to give me messages was completely outside of the box of my beliefs, but I felt something inside me begin to stir, to come alive. It is so difficult to explain. Just the possibility that God cared about me caused me to begin to feel alive again, like a flame had been ignited in my soul.

During our conversation, he invited me to come to his home in St. Petersburg, just across the bay from Tampa, so that we could talk in person. Gary told me that God directed him not to charge me, so there would be no fee for our meeting. We agreed on a time to meet the next day. After just his brief conversation, I felt different somehow, I felt lighter. Like there were answers coming. That lighter feeling inside me was what I have come to understand as the awakening of the Light of Truth within us. The Light, as I have now realized, was drawing me back Home.

The next day, as I drove across the Howard Franklin Bridge from Tampa to St. Petersburg, the sun glistened off the Tampa Bay waters, and I felt at peace, something I had not experienced in a long while. The conflict of relationship had taken a heavy toll on my spirit and peace of mind. I was stressed and anxious-- so much so that I was getting muscle twitches in my legs that caused me enough concern to see a doctor, who could find nothing wrong. Driving across the bridge over Tampa Bay was the beginning of the journey of awakening into the Presence of God. In fact, now, over twenty years later, I drive across the same bridge to St Petersburg every week to teach *A Course in Miracles* at Wings Bookstore.

Even more interesting is that just recently (2019) I came across, by accident, an old Spanish map at the New York public library from the 1500's that labeled Tampa Bay as *"Bahia Del Espiritu Santo"*. In English, it is simply *"The Bay of the Holy Spirit."* On the top part of the map it says: *"A Plan of Bahia del Santo on the West Side of Florida."* In English, *"A Plan of the Holy Spirit on the West Side of Florida."*

Looking back, could that be part of the reason I was beginning to feel better as I crossed the bay to Gary's house? I arrived at Gary's beautiful Tierra Verde home at the appointed time, climbed a steep flight of stairs to his front door, rang the bell and waited for the door to open.

I am standing in the Is-ness of God and realizing
that where I am, God's grace is my sufficiency in all things.
—Joel Goldsmith

11

UNCERTAINTY IS THE DREAM

TWO MINUTES AGO, I asked Jesus what to write next. He said write about what motivated me to call Gary in the first place. He said to remind those who will read this book that I was driven largely by the concept of "uncertainty." I was deeply uncertain about everything. I was uncertain about my income, relationships, the welfare of my children and my future life. I was motivated to talk to Gary because I was uncertain, which feels threatening and produces fear. I was in deep fear. Uncertainty is hell.

As Jesus was instructing me just now to write about my uncertainty and fear, an unsolicited email message from an insurance company flashed across the screen of the computer I am typing on.

The message read: *"Help protect your income from UNCERTAINTY."*

I have to smile at the guidance of Jesus. He knows that the lawyer in me entertains at least a little bit of doubt just in case I may be hearing inaccurately. As a lawyer, whenever possible, I double check everything in case I missed something important to the success of the matter I am working on. The law is full of nuances which can become traps and mistakes. I know I have created more work and concern that has been necessary over the years. I will often ask for a physical sign as confirmation of guidance.

The insurance company email that said "Help protect your income from "UNCERTAINTY" was one of those confirmations of his guidance. Confirmations are very helpful and will come when we ask and trust. I have become more and more trusting and confident in his presence and constant guidance. As *A Course in Miracles* states:

Lesson 135 If I defend myself I am attacked

Your Present trust in Him is the defense that promises a future undisturbed, without a trace of sorrow, and with joy that constantly increases, as this life becomes a holy instant, set in time, but heeding only immortality. Let no defenses but your present trust direct the future, and this life becomes a meaningful encounter with the truth that only your defenses would conceal.

Through years of study and contemplation of *A Course in Miracles*, I have come to understand that uncertainty rules the dream we believe is our life. As many of us already know, or at least suspect, we in fact see, with our human body eyes, only an "appearance" of what we have come to think of and accept as "reality." The dream appearance images or moving pictures are not the Creation of our Loving Creator. This dream was not designed by what we think of as God. Love, the very essence of God, could not possibly have created an environment with such widely differing characteristics and traits that don't exist within Love.

Would a God of Love, that is neither male nor female, have created bodies that are opposites of each other in both form and thought? Since the beginning of history and to this very day, men and women have been in conflict. Adam and Eve had a conflict from the get-go. Sure, there are seemingly wonderful love stories, but even within those stories, there is a world of conflict. God did not create conflict. God did not create bodies that oppose each other.

And then as if this basic conflict of male and female isn't enough, "He" created black skin, white skin, brown skin, tall people, fat people, skinny people, gay people, straight people, poor people, rich people, Asians, Caucasians, Africans, Hispanics and on and on, oh my!

After all that creative creating, He saw the mess of potential conflict he stirred up. So he said to Himself, "Crap, I really messed that up." Then He made up some story about catching us eating from the sacred apple tree as an excuse to get rid of his messed-up creation. He kicked us out of the Kingdom of Peace, locked the gate and waved goodbye, "Good luck; you'll need it. And remember to pray to me asking me to solve all those conflicts I created."

Love did not create not-love. Conflict is not-love. The world of conflict is a world of images made by the ego. The ego then convinces us that *we are the images* that we "think we think":

ACIM Lesson 15 My thoughts are images I have made.

It is because the thoughts you think you think appear as images that you do not recognize them (the images) as nothing. You think you think them, and so you think you see them. This is how your "seeing" was made. This is the function you have given your body's eyes. It is not seeing. It is image making. It takes the place of seeing, replacing vision with illusions.

God, Being Perfect Love, created us in Love's own image. What is that image? Love. Pure Innocent Holy Joyful Warm Radiant Perfect Love. For what is an image? When we look in a mirror or look into the clear calm surface of water, we can see our image. We can see what we think of as our self in the image that is reflected back. When we look in the mirror, we don't see a reflection of a kitty cat or a tree. We "see" what we believe is our self, the human face we have come to believe is our self. As a human body that we believe we are, it's not possible to see an image in the mirror that's not a body.

In the same way, Love was not able to Create an image of anything other than Love's own image. Perfection's own image. Joy's own image. Peace's own image. Kindness' own image. Holiness' own image. Innocence's own image. God's own image.

That image is you and me. That image is US. That image is Christ. That image is not the human body appearing as us. It is the Spirit Us that Love created like unto Itself. Love cannot create hate. Love cannot create fear. Love cannot create uncertainty. Love cannot create cruelty. Love cannot create misery and suffering. Love cannot create something unlike itself. It cannot create differences and separate things and lacks and sickness and pain.

You see, Love cannot create hell. Differences, degrees, varieties and "space between" imagined things is hell. But the little self that we believe we are can imagine a hell-filled dream world that is completely separate, (and has no existence) from the Divine Mind of God--the Divine Mind of Love that created us. The dream world images that we "see," whether those images are of earthquakes or sunsets, tranquil countryside or chaotic city streets, gently rolling ocean waves or hurricanes and tidal waves, are all false images NOT created by our Father. Not created by Love. Jesus calls the images *hallucinations:*

ACIM Text Chapter 20 VIII 7

*Judgment is but a toy, a whim, the senseless means to play the idle game of death in your imagination. But vision sets all things right, bringing them gently within the kindly sway of Heaven's Laws. <u>What if you recognized this world is a hallucination</u>? What if you really understood that **you** made it up? What if you realized that those who seem to walk about in it, to sin and die, attack and murder and destroy themselves, are wholly unreal? Could you have faith in what you see, if you accepted this? And would you see it?*

Hallucinations disappear when they are recognized for what they are. This is the healing and the remedy. Believe them not and they are gone. And all you need to do is recognize that you did this. Once you accept this simple fact and take unto yourself the power you gave them, you are released from them. One thing is sure; hallucinations serve a purpose, and when that purpose is no longer held, they disappear. Therefore, the question never is whether you want them, but always, do you want the purpose that they serve? This world seems to hold out many purposes, each different and with different values. Yet they are all the same. Again, there is no order; only a seeming hierarchy of values.

Only two purposes are possible. And one is sin, the other holiness. Nothing is in between, and which you choose determines what you see. For what you see is merely how you elect to meet your goal. Hallucinations serve to meet the goal of madness.

As I waited at Gary's door that day in late '90s, my uncertain mind felt a sense of hope. I don't even know why I felt hopeful. I was seeking help from someone who was not a priest. This was out of character for me, but it felt right and good. I just knew, perhaps on an unacknowledged or unrecognized spiritual level, that the Light calling me back to Truth was growing brighter, calling me to come back "home."

I had not yet met Gary, nor had I seen any pictures of him, so I had no idea of what he looked like. When he answered the door, I was completely thrown off guard. What a surprise! I really don't know what my expectation was, but I know for sure that I was not expecting a man dressed entirely in white from head to toe with big snow-white hair! He had a huge smile, a southern accent and a happy face. I couldn't help but stare, while pretending I really didn't notice. I thought he must have realized how odd he looked. But despite his out-of-the-ordinary appearance, I felt comfortable in his company. He was unbelievably friendly, with a gentle laugh that put me at ease right away. It was like meeting someone I had known all of my life. There was immediate ease and peace.

Later, as we became very good friends, he told me that God had told him how to dress and appear. As I got to know Gary, I realized the most important thing to him was to do God's Will and follow His guidance regardless of how silly it may seem or how much it may or may not make sense. As the years passed in our friendship, I found this to be his most admirable characteristic. Doing God's Will. Listening to His Voice as best as he could and then doing as he was told and guided to do. I came to realize that the Voice of God was his guiding Light and it became obvious to me that it was the only "thing" that was important to him.

I found out and realized all this later. Back then, I was following him up the stairs into his living room that was full of candles, giant gemstones and Angel statues. He invited me to sit while he got some water for us from the kitchen. I was nervous and yet there was also an overwhelming sense that something good was about to happen. I felt a happiness deep inside. He came back in the living room and sat on a big beautiful chair that looked like it came out of a European castle. After he settled in, we made casual conversation.

Then he began to "read" me. He absolutely blew me away!

In this dream life, I was born in Oneida New York on July 9,1959. Because of my fathers' job, we moved about every four or five years. From New York, we moved to Somerville, New Jersey, then to Pittsburgh Pennsylvania and in 1971, to Tampa, Florida.

Most of my formative years were spent during the sixties and seventies, witnessing and listening to the dawning of the age of Aquarius. Even though we lived out in the wooded green new suburbs of the northeast, I was captivated by the emerging new world of hippies, war protest, peace, love and "far out" fashion. The world around me seemed to be experiencing an awakening of sorts.

In contrast to this new world of "free love," I spent my days during the school year in strict Catholic schools, fearing God and the nuns with rulers and a dead Jesus hanging from their waists. And at the same time as experiencing the fear of God, trying to understand this guy Jesus who seemed to be such a loving soul. Why was God to be feared, and yet his allegedly "only son" was to be loved. We were told that Jesus loved us very much, but Jesus' father, the God of fear, wasn't so thrilled with the sinners that we are. In order to slap us out of our sinfulness, as the story goes, God sent his son Jesus to earth. Once on earth, God carefully planned his son's torture and bloody death. Then, because of this bloody insane sacrifice of his son, everyone was "saved." So, this God that I am supposed to love is teaching me that killing and sacrificing a body, especially your own son, is a positive thing for the world and a fine example to emulate in my life. Are you kidding? On what planet does that make sense?

Confusion upon confusion. It seemed that God was trying to scare the living crap out of me by having his son crucified even though he had done nothing wrong. God apparently wanted us all to realize that He was all powerful and very willing to sacrifice his son in a most gruesome way so that we as sinners would fear God and behave ourselves or else!

The story is that Jesus sacrificed his own life so that we would be spared God's wrath. Jesus soaked up all of our despicableness as born sinners. He saved us from the wrath of God. He saved us from God sending us to eternal hell.

It's very clear that this story, no matter how one tries to twist and turn it to make sense of it, is a flat-out distortion of Truth. It is a lie about Love. It is crap. It is baloney.

Stop now. Right now, stop believing this story. Just stop it. Now.

In *A Course In Miracles* Jesus says in no uncertain terms, **Chapter 6 I. The message of the crucifixion:**

I elected, for your sake and mine, to demonstrate that the most outrageous assault, as judged by the ego, does not matter. As the world judges these things, but not as God knows them, I was betrayed, abandoned, beaten, torn and finally killed. It was clear that this was only because of the projection of others onto me, since I had not harmed anyone and had healed many.

The message of the crucifixion is perfectly clear:

Teach only love, for that is what you are.

*If you interpret the crucifixion in any other way, you are using it as a weapon of assault rather than as the **call for peace** for which it was intended.*

Because *ACIM* wasn't available to the world in my youth, I was stuck pondering these things that didn't make sense. Even at that young age, no matter what spin religion put on the story in order to justify or try to make it seem like a believable story, each explanation became more and more downright silly, to put it mildly. As I would come to learn from *ACIM*, Truth is simple and needs no convoluted stories to be True.

ACIM lesson 152⋯. The power of decision is my own.

No one can suffer loss unless it be his own decision. No one suffers pain except his choice elects this state for him. No one can grieve nor fear nor think him sick unless these are the outcomes that he wants. And no one dies without his own consent. Nothing occurs but represents your wish, and nothing is omitted that you choose. Here is your world, complete in all details. Here is its whole reality for you. And it is only here salvation is.

You may believe that this position is extreme, and too inclusive to be true. Yet can truth have exceptions? If you have the gift of everything, can loss be real? Can pain be part of peace, or grief of joy? Can fear and sickness enter a mind where love and perfect holiness abide? Truth must be all inclusive, if it be truth at all. Accept no opposites and no exceptions, for to do so is to contradict the truth entirely.

Salvation is the recognition that the truth is true, and nothing else is true.

I was hoping, and somehow felt, that Gary Spivey would help me with the confusion in my life.

There is no substitute for Peace.
What God creates has no alternative.
– ACIM Chapter 24

12

LET ME SHOW YOU THE WAY

AS AN ALTAR BOY at Holy Trinity Church in
Pittsburgh, I would serve mass in the early morning
before school several times a month. It seemed so
dreary, somber and repetitive. It was serious and
stifling. Sometimes I earned extra money serving at
funerals. The money wasn't bad for a boy my age, but
the experience made me sick to my stomach. The smell
of incense combined with the lack of joy was scary. I
couldn't help wondering if any of the dogma had any
truth at all. For sure, I knew Jesus was real. I knew he
lived a life to teach us love. But I also sensed that his
story, or his real reason for walking amongst us, had
been distorted by churches, religions and politics long
ago. Something inside told me that the lies about who he
was and why he came need to be corrected.

I distinctly remember my father taking me to see the movie "The Greatest Story Ever Told." I was about six years old, and it was just my dad and me. This movie had a dramatic effect on me. I remember the crucifixion scene like it was yesterday. And I remember crying and feeling sad. I was so incredibly confused. All that I kept saying to myself through the tears I tried to hide was "Why did they have to kill him? He did nothing wrong." This thought kept repeating over and over in my mind. The crucifixion of Jesus just made no sense to me even as a six-year-old child. "Why?" I asked myself. "Why would God send His child to be killed?"

The story just never made sense to me. Then I read the "Greatest Book Ever Written" ···. *A Course In Miracles*. This beautiful blue book finally answered my questions about the truth of Jesus' crucifixion. It will answer all of our questions. It will explain to us why we even have questions. For when we think about it, to have a question is to be in a state of uncertainty. To be in a state of uncertainty is to be in a state--or in a feeling--of being separate or apart from God.

The separateness or apartness feeling that Jesus speaks to us of is not unlike the apartness that we feel or perceive when we are not in the same room with another person. For instance, in the dream "reality," when I am in the kitchen with my wife, we are together. We are not apart. But when she leaves the kitchen and goes to sit in the living room, we are now separated. We are in separate rooms. We are no longer looking at the same surroundings. I am experiencing the seeing of the sink and dirty dishes and the coffee maker. She is having a different experience apart from mine. She experiences the couch and pillows and magazines. We are now separated. In this separated state, we have different thoughts that run through our seemingly separate minds. We now, on the level of the dream appearances, are experiencing different and separate worlds. I am not certain of her experiences and she not mine. There is no longer a unity of experience. We are not both having the experience of the kitchen.

This is a very simplistic example of separation in this world. On a grand scale, the male gender is having a different experience than the female gender. My economic status is having a different, separate experience, apart from your economic status. Your ethnic background is not the same experience as mine. My country has different interests than your country. And on and on it goes. My religion is separate from yours; it teaches separate, different concepts.

Differences separate us into me and 'other-than-me.' We develop interests separate and apart from one another in the dream. The perception of separateness and difference generates threat and fear. The looking out at a face or gender or religion that I am not identified with in the dream causes a trigger of uncertainty within the human mind, or what we call the ego. I am not looking at 'me,' so I am not sure or certain of what I am viewing. This can arouse fear.

The ego looks through the human eyes which are designed to not see the Truth of us and sees something different than itself. This causes an uneasiness within. It must then analyze and make judgments. Is this person safe to be around? Is she going to harm me?

For instance, the Christian ego eye sees the Jewish man, "Mmm," the ego mind says, "He has different beliefs than mine." The personal self then can feel a subtle threat to its thoughts. Uncertainty arises. There is not perfect peace of mind. Differences in appearances, however subtle and innocent, disturb perfect peace.

 Uneasiness and uncertainty sound the alarm of defenses and tell us clearly, through the voice of 'not peace' (the ego) that we are in fact different and apart. Not quite the same. Not with quite the same interests. And it whispers, "If his nature is not quite the same as mine, can I trust him?" We. as a dreaming world, are seemingly getting better at overlooking differences, but the ego will never let them go completely.

A man and a woman meet. There are some sparks. Together with those sparks are the obvious differences. Right away, right from the beginning, there are two separate, different genders thinking different thoughts. They are not the same. Each has something to protect. Defenses fly up. Caution, another name for fear, speaks loudly. The ego says "He may hurt me, she may deceive. We better be careful, we better be cautious, we better be afraid and on guard." On the human dream appearance level, it makes sense to be cautious and careful. But, and this is the big but, we are *not* on the dream level. We, in Truth, dwell in the Kingdom of Heaven. Yet the dream is seemingly so real, that we react as if we are not in the presence of God. We act as if we could be separate from our Creator. We react as if we believe that what the human personal eye seems to see is real. We seem to live in the dream, when in fact, we live only within the Kingdom of Heaven, the Divine Loving Mind of God. Not the brain of a God with a human-like body. Banish that image. Rather, remember the feeling of being nurtured within a warm glowing cocoon of eternal safety, where a want or a need or a desire is not known, for it has already been fulfilled by our Creator.

Now, this very moment in time as I write this, my cell phone just sounded a loud obnoxious alarm. I picked up my phone and read the message flashing across the screen:

"Emergency Alert: 911 phone outage in unincorporated Hillsborough County, for emergencies dial⋯"

Jesus again confirming what I just wrote above about the **alarm** that is sounded within us when we live in and perceive a world of being apart and separate. There is an uneasiness, a subtle, or often not-so-subtle anxiety that is the alarm of fear. It is the voice of the ego. It's the thought system of the separate personal self whose special, personal interests are being threatened by the separate, different person body that I see. "Be ready," the ego says, "to defend yourself." And we do it in hurtful words, in the hurtful withholding of love and sometimes with nuclear weapons. This morning I was led by Jesus to read lesson 167 again:

ACIM Lesson 167 There is one life and that I share with God

*In this world there appears to be a state that is life's opposite. You call it death. Yet we have learned that the idea of death takes many forms. It is the one idea that underlies all feelings that are not supremely happy. It is the **ALARM** to which you give response of any kind that is not perfect joy. All sorrow, loss, anxiety and suffering and pain, even a little sigh of weariness, a slight discomfort, or the merest frown, acknowledge death. And thus deny you live.*

I am hopeful that the reader will be blessed by my sharing the experiences in the dream life of Paul that point to the Truth of the Miracle of Perfect Love, our Holiness. My prayer for us is that we remember our Holy Innocent Self. My prayer is that we gently melt back into the Light of Holy Peace. And I pray that we accept the Love of God back into the Heart of our Awareness. That we accept the Holy Peace that we are and that we remember our way back. It, The Way Back Home, is within us. I pray that we remember with Jesus. I pray that my journey has followed in the footsteps of Jesus and that within my journey, yours will be lighted and perhaps be a bit gentler, a bit smoother than mine has been. In *A Course in Miracles*, Jesus promises that his was the last useless journey to the cross. He has kept his promise. Mine has been way gentler by comparison to his. I have done my best to trust him. My prayer for you is to trust him, too.

When I was a child, just about every time I went to church, I got a stomachache. Rarely did I feel like I wasn't going to throw up. I am serious. Something about church just didn't feel right. It wasn't the people, or really even the priests, who for the most part were well-intentioned and doing the best they could with what they had been taught. It just didn't feel like a happy place. It didn't sound like a happy message I was hearing. It was about sin and death and confession and God's judgment and praying that God won't kill me. Or praying that my school bus doesn't slide off the icy road into the ravine on the way home from school before going to weekly confession.

The only relief I got from the heaviness of the Catholic Church was in my love of playing baseball and wandering through the hills and woods that were always at my disposal. I especially loved hiking through the woods alone in the wintertime when there was a deep snow. For years, although I had many neighborhood friends to play with, I found myself wandering off by myself.

In the summer, I loved getting on my green bike with a white banana seat and raised handlebars. I would ride up and down the surrounding streets, climbing a hill with all my strength, then zooming down the other side flying so fast that my heart would soar.

In the wintertime, I would take my sled out onto the snowy hills, endlessly trudging up and down the hill until exhausted. The hike up the hill was worth the thrill of the ride down. This I would learn, was a life lesson. The work and discipline of studying and reading *A Course in Miracles* has a payoff, the thrill of the ride down the other side of suffering. The thrill of finding that the truth in ACIM, as it is integrated into our daily life dream, is the payoff. It is the payoff of ending the suffering and misery that we have come to expect as "part of life." This expectation has been reinforced by religious teachings that tell us we are sinners and that we are flawed. Misery and suffering are the result of the sin of Adam and Eve that has been passed along to each child born into this world. When that story of sin is mistakenly accepted and perpetuated, the goal of life is to be good, act right, go to church services and confess sins, so that one day, on the day of our 'death,' God may judge us worthy to enter heaven and end our misery.

I am the second oldest of eight children born into the story of a Catholic Irish–Italian family. As I wrote above, all of us have biblical names. My parents are Peter and Mary. My grandfathers were both Josephs. One of my grandmothers was Mary. My older brother is

Peter. I am Paul. After me is Mary Jane, Matthew, Mark, Luke, John and David. We pretty much have the New Testament covered.

With such a large family, there was always a lot of commotion. So wandering off into the woods to explore and hike by myself was an escape into the quiet and stillness of nature. The snowy winter was especially magical in the woods. It was so silent and white. There in the hills outside of Pittsburgh, I had my first experience with the Presence, the Power of Peace and the Perfect Love.

One snowy Saturday afternoon, I was drawn to my favorite place in the woods. It was only about a 15-minute hike, but it was quite hilly, and the snow was deep. That particular day, as I look back upon it now, felt like I was being drawn to a light. I didn't know why I was going into the woods that day, I just knew I had to go.

I arrived at my favorite place. It was a deep ravine with what appeared to be an old riverbed at least 30 yards wide. Across the riverbed there were fallen trees. One huge fallen tree had formed a bridge across the riverbed that I could actually walk across. Underneath the tree was a small winding creek that babbled rhythmically through the broken openings in the ice. This was a pure, peaceful, white silent place for me to be alone. Again, looking back at myself at the age of about 12, it is magical to realize that I was led to something that would take me a lifetime to understand.

That day, there was several feet of fresh snow on the ground. The sky was a brilliant winter blue, and the sun was high and bright, casting beautiful shadows and beams of light down through the tree-lined riverbed ravine, my secret wonderland of peace. There was pure still silence. Complete cocooned softness of the stillness of snow.

I was drawn to lie down in the snow beside the trickling stream. I remember having the thought, "What am I doing? What if I fall asleep and freeze to death?" But there was an irresistible urge, a peaceful presence that beckoned me to close my eyes and rest. My fears of freezing to death quickly passed, and I soon fell into a deep, deep peace that felt like a "floating" peace that I can still feel to this day.

And as I fell deeper into the Presence of Peace, It spoke these words to me:

"Let Me show you The Way," It said. "Let Me show you The Way Home."

For some reason, I wasn't startled by the voice I heard. I guess I wasn't even startled by the fact that I even heard a voice in the middle of the snowy woods. It was not a deep booming voice by any means. Rather, it was a gentle, almost 'silent' voice that seemed most natural. It came from somewhere within me, filling me with peace and stillness. I remember staying with it for as long as I could. It felt like a beautiful warm magnet that I didn't want to pull away from. I didn't want to open my eyes and be separate from this beautiful peaceful Presence.

ACIM Chapter 9 V

The only meaningful contribution the healer can make is to present an example of one whose direction has been changed FOR him, and who no longer believes in nightmares.

After what turned out to be about an hour, but felt like only a few minutes, I opened my eyes, sat up in the snow and looked around. I could still feel the peaceful Presence, but it seemed to be ebbing away in its intensity. The northeastern afternoon sun was beginning to set already, casting a beautiful glow through the trees, resting softly upon the pure white snow. Gentle snow flurries had begun to fall, and the warmth of the sun began to fade. Time to make my way home, I thought. Time to reluctantly leave this little piece of Heaven. It would be dinner soon, and I didn't want to be late.

It wasn't until I wrote about this experience that it dawned on me that my thought at twelve years of age would be the guiding thought of the Prince of Peace throughout my life. Even now, right this very moment, I have tears as I write these words because I can feel the strength of his promise never to leave me without comfort. Ultimately, it is the Love God, that comes through the Holy Spirit. These tears are the remembrance and the realization that Love has never left my side as promised. Within the dream of this life, Love was with me that day in the woods and it was Love, through Jesus and the Christ we are, that spoke the words, *"Let Me Show You The Way Home."*

What appeared to be my earthly thoughts of "time to make my way home for dinner" have a meaning on another level now. For what was planted within my mind on the path of this dream life, was the story of the Prodigal Son that Jesus spoke of when he walked upon the earth. It is time to make our way back to our Father's House, where He has a feast prepared for us. It's time to make our way home.

My experience that afternoon, unknown to me at the time, was the call to make my way home to the Reality of Heaven. It was time to put aside the dream of being a human being, and to come Home to the Truth of who I am and Where I am.

We share this dream of not being aware that we are still in Heaven and still one with the Love of God. We have become lost in the nightmare dream. *A Course in Miracles* is the road map that helps us wake up to Heaven quicker, gentler and easier. As we wake up to the Truth, all of which is found in *A Course in Miracles*, we naturally head towards the Light of Home. We have all wandered far from Home. This wandering, though, has only taken place in our minds. It only seems to have happened. It only seems that we have left our natural state of Peace in God and wandered into a nightmare where everything is fearful, limited and full of scarcity.

Look at the word that the dream uses. Scarcity. It means a limitation, not enough of something. Lacking wholeness and completeness. And what state of mind, what emotion does that produce? Fear.

SCARE—CITY. We seem to live in a city, a world, that produces nothing but scariness. Nothing but fear. Fortunately, fear is not real. We made it up. Only love is real. And it is not possible for both Love and fear to exist in the same space or in the same thought. We can only hold one thought at a time. We cannot hold, at the same instant, both a thought of fear and a thought of Love and Safety. God and fear cannot coexist. Only God Is. Only Love Is. Only God Exists. Only Perfect Love Exists. Nothing else can be at all.

It is critical to recognize that threat—fear is the veil that hides Peace. It is critical to recognize that Peace is the only Reality. This Reality of Peace and all it contains IS the Kingdom of Heaven.

Lesson 52 (6) I am upset because I see what is not there.

Reality is never frightening. It is impossible that it could upset me. Reality brings only perfect peace. When I am upset, it is always because I have replaced Reality with illusions I made up. The illusions are upsetting because

I have given them "reality" and thus regard Reality as illusion. Nothing in God's creation is affected in any way by this confusion of mine. I am always upset by nothing.

Let this short lesson be a trigger that reminds us to choose Reality, to Choose the Power of Peace. When we notice our self in fear, here is a prayer inspired by Jesus:

"I am feeling fear. But Jesus says Reality is never ever fearful. I must be making this situation, event, person or thought Real. I must be giving it Reality and therefore it deserves my allegiance and obedience. I must be seeing it as important and requiring my attention and reaction. The emotion that this causes me to feel must be real and I must do as the emotion instructs. I feel weak and helpless. But Jesus assures me that Reality is never frightening. So, if I am frightened and feel helpless, I let it go as best as I can. I forgive it as best as I can. I rest in the strength my Christ Self defenselessness. As best as I can, I see and feel my own Holiness instead. I rest here in the Reality of my Holiness and Peace. I feel God's enveloping Perfect Love, Peace and Eternal Safety."

Try to hold a fear thought at the same time as holding thought of happiness or peace. You tried. You can't do it. You can only hold one thought at a time. Decide now, right now, for the rest of your dream life, to only ever to hold the Thought of the Defenselessness of Peace and Perfect Love. This is Reality, the Kingdom of Heaven.

ACIM Lesson 34. I could see peace instead of this (what I see/feel now)

Peace of mind is clearly an internal matter. It must begin with your own thoughts, and then extend outward. It is from your peace of mind that a peaceful perception of the world arises.

I could see peace in this situation instead of what I now see in it.

I can replace my feelings of depression, anxiety or worry with peace.

So now, as I relate this story of lying in a peaceful state in the snow, I can see the metaphorical nature of the experience. I can see what it was pointing towards. It was time for the prodigal son to wake up and go home to peace and to sit at the table of plenty.

I made my way through the knee-deep snow and the fading light, toward home. Up the hills and out of the woods. As I approached the outside basement door to our home, I heard that gentle voice remind me again;

"Let Me show you the way home."

Certainly, in my 12-year-old mind, the voice had shown me the way home. Even though I loved wandering in the woods, especially in the winter, there was a part of me that was always a bit concerned about remembering my way home. So, my 12-year-old mind was glad I was guided home that day through the snow and fading light. I told myself that that voice was there just to protect me from freezing to death in the woods, kind of like a guardian angel. I smiled to myself and just tucked away the whole experience. I didn't really think about it after that day and pretty much forgot about it.

I now know that my wandering in the woods, looking for peace, is symbolic for wandering in the dream world of appearances, looking for peace and happiness. Although in fact my walks in the snow-white silent woods were very peaceful, it was not Reality. But it did help point me in Heaven's direction. It was a peace so deep, silent and pure that it spoke to me. Peace said, *"Let me show you the way home."*

Although I am sure It was always with me, I didn't hear that voice again so clearly until many years later.

Although you appear in earthly form Your essence is pure consciousness.
You are the fearless guardian of Divine Light.
– Rumi

13

OUR SACRED ROBE OF LIGHT

AS I SAT WITH Gary Spivey the day that I met him for
the first time, my thoughts were on the turmoil of my
life circumstances. Truthfully, I didn't know what in the
world I was doing there. I can just say it felt good to be
there with him. It felt like meeting an old friend that I
hadn't seen in years but had thought fondly about many
times. Despite not knowing Gary yet as a trusted
friend, the feeling within me was bubbling over with joy,
an inner smile that I could not contain. Joy. Yes, I just
felt pure joy to be there with him.

The first thing he said was that I was a beautiful bright
white light. He said whiter and brighter than he had
ever seen. He repeated this several times to make sure
I understood, emphasizing the clarity in which he could
see my light and its bright glow. He said that the Angels
wanted me to understand the brilliance of my light.

At that time in my spiritual awakening, I did not know what he was referring to when he spoke of my light. I didn't have any experience at all with spirit light or psychics or being aware of anything other than what my human eyes could see. And yet even though I did not understand the seeing of my light intellectually, I remember having a feeling of recognizing the light again. It was like when someone reminds you of a time you shared together, the memory of which can light you up with a smile. We come alive again, so to speak, within that happy memory. We light up.

And so it was when Gary spoke to me of my bright light. It was like a happy memory, and it felt wonderful.

As I said, what prompted me to call Gary in the first place was the uncertainty of my life circumstances. Everything was up in the air. I was worn out and tired from all the struggle and strain related to trying to save the marriage. My physical health caused me concern as I was experiencing muscle spasms and twitching in my legs and arms which had caused me to seek help from doctors. They could find nothing wrong. I was convinced that I had a neuromuscular disease. Recently, one of my neighbors, a young father, had been stricken with ALS, which confined him to a wheelchair, eventually causing his death at a young age, leaving a wife and small children.

I didn't tell Gary about my physical symptoms when I sat down with him, but I was carrying the worried thought that there was something wrong with me. At the same time, I didn't want to know, as I was afraid of what he may say. He gently said, "Well, let me see, let me take a look at what is going on with you."

It's funny now, but I remember thinking, ok, how exactly do I let you 'look'? What do I do to allow this to happen? Should I think certain thoughts? Should I have no thoughts? While these thoughts were swirling through me, he was silent, sort of looking off somewhere at something I couldn't see. I can't explain it at all, but I had a feeling of safety as he sat there allowing himself to see or sense what was going on.

Finally, after what seemed like the longest time, but was only a minute or so, he smiled and laughingly said, "There is not a thing wrong with you; why are you running around to doctors? Nothing is wrong with you. But I will tell what is wrong in your life that is causing this."

He said God was telling him that all of the stress and strain that was associated with my marriage and my feeling of believing I should be able to fix what just was not possible to fix was causing a drain on my Light and health. He explained that over a lifetime, I had accepted the idea from the world that there was something wrong with me. He explained that darkness was trying to put out my Light. He explained, in very simple terms, what he meant as darkness. In his language, he explained that darkness tries to block the Light that we are. The darkness works through us when we don't stay aware of the Light through meditation. Darkness also works through those around us so that we are, in a very literal sense, attacked by darkness. This blocks the Light and preoccupies us with problems and worries, so much so that we can become sick and depressed.

He explained that there were many bright Lights here on earth to light it up with God's Light so that we could make it all Light. He told me so many things that were going on in my life, things that he could not possibly have known. Through my Angels and Spirit, he told me how to deal with all the earthly issues that were arising and exactly how to handle them, which lifted so much burden from my mind.

One of the other highlights was when one of my deceased grandmothers came through and spoke about things that we shared when I was a little boy that only my grandmother would have known about. I was just in awe. All the talk of Light and darkness had shifted my outlook. He gave me very helpful, very practical advice on how to handle my life situation which was full of the fear of uncertainty.

We spoke for almost three hours. Much of the time was spent on my angels emphasizing the importance of recognizing my Light and that I had been brought there by the Light. He called it "Christ led." I was led there by the Light of Christ. Again, all of this was entirely new to me. I somehow understood him on a spiritual level. There was a part of me that seemed to come alive again.

When Gary looked at me with a confident smile and said, "You are a bright Light, and the world needs more people like you," I literally could feel a huge burden lifted from me. Like a giant weight was removed from my mind that was blocking my Light. Later I realized that from the very beginning of this dream life, many of my dream characters told me, in one way or another, that there was something wrong with me. Having this lie lifted felt like a miracle. It is impossible to describe the feeling of being told that you are valuable, when your whole life has been about "battling" the world of religion and relationships that do their best to convince you that you are flawed, not loved and there is something wrong with you.

I know now that it was my dream of not-love. I would come to understand I had called forth this dream. I would also come to understand that I could choose the happy dream instead, dreamed by Christ to lead me home.

From the unified perspective of the truth in *A Course in Miracles*, I now know the meaning of all of those feelings and how the projected world hypnotizes us into believing its lies about our Real Identity. Keep in mind though, (as I would come to learn later from ACIM) that we projected a false guilt onto the screen of the world to be acted out by our dream characters. We have done this to ourselves. The world of ego personal selves wants to kill the Christ that we are:

ACIM Clarification of Terms 2. The Ego-The Miracle

This was the ego---all the cruel hate, the need for vengeance and the cries of pain, the fear of dying and the urge to kill, the botherless illusion and the self that seemed alone in all the universe. This terrible mistake about yourself the miracle corrects as gently as a loving mother sings her child to rest. Is not a song like this what you would hear? Would it not answer all you thought to ask, and even make the question meaningless?

There was part of me that was at least partially reawakening, a part of me that did not find the feeling that I am a bright Light to be odd. Rather, it was hinting, a reminder of why I am here. I certainly did not know that at that time. But I clearly see it now. We are the Light of God. We are here to be the Light, and by remembering that we are the Light, darkness, ignorance and unawareness of God will dissolve. Darkness, the world appearances that seem to be real, will be unable to exist in the Light of who we are. The awakening is all about the recalling of who we are.

ACIM Lesson 61 I am the light of the world.

Who is the light of the world except God's Son? (as We were Created) This, then, is merely a statement of the truth about yourself. It is the opposite of a statement of pride, of arrogance, or of self-deception. It does not describe the self-concept that you have made. (the little personal self) It does not refer to any of the characteristics with which you have endowed your idols. It refers to you as you were created by God. It (I am the light of the world) simply states the truth.

It is helpful to realize that the "world" that Jesus speaks of is the false dream world that we seem to see in our minds. Holy Spirit is inspiring me that this lesson is really saying:

"I am as God created me. I am Light. In my mind I seem to see appearances of struggle, misery and fear. But I remember that I am none of that which appears in my mind. I am the Light of holiness, which is what I now choose to be aware of instead of the world of misery and darkness in my mind. I am Light. I see my Light. I feel my Light. I stand firmly in my Holy Light."

I didn't comprehend all of this at the time I first met with Gary. I just knew I felt like a giant weight had been lifted from my shoulders. I felt alive again, optimistic and hopeful. I felt there was a darkness that had been replaced by something called "Light." I have come to realize that Light is Truth, and a lifting away of the darkness leaves Peace in its wake. It was so joyful to know that I had a life ahead of me that was filled with Light. For the first time in years and years, I felt a sense of confidence and peace return.

As I was about to leave Gary's home, he looked out the window as if he was staring at something. He smiled and said, "God just told me that we are going to be lifelong friends and that you will have a wonderful, "magical" life." He went on to say that I was to call him any time I needed to. There would be no charge ever. That he was instructed by God to help me whenever and wherever I needed help.

I didn't ask why I would need his help. I just had a deep feeling that I had found a friend and that he would look out for my best interests. That this friend had my back. It had been so long since I felt that way. It was the Light of God working through Gary.

Shortly thereafter, as I contemplated moving forward with my divorce and life, what I have come to know as my Christ Presence, or the I Am That I Am, whispered again to me in the midst of the stillness of the night on New Year's Eve. I was by myself with my two daughters at Disney World. After they were asleep, I stepped outside for a moment to enjoy the silent night sky. This Presence of Peace said, *"Even though what lies ahead of you is unknown to you, do not fear; it will be unlike what lies behind you. Do not fear what is yet unknown to you, and do not look back."* With these words my mind was set. I would move forward with my life.

Those silent, encouraging words spoken to me in the stillness of the night instilled a deep sense of confidence. Those words were spoken from The Presence of Love and Peace. With that feeling, I went to bed with a smile on my face, not knowing what was yet to come, but knowing that all would be well. The Light of Peace, with whom we share the same inheritance, has a never-ending patience in the task of turning us back to the Awareness of the eternal Presence of God that is literally the "within-ness" of who we are. This "within-ness" is the same as the Pureness of our Holiness. Holy Within-ness. One with God. This is our Home. This radiant joyful "feeling" is the Love of God. This is how or what God feels like. Feeling that Joy is the remembering of Home. Grace, pure flowing Grace. Smooth and warm, flowing through our very being. This is *where* we live. This is the Life of Love. This is the very heart of God. The Grace of God.

We can and do feel God. Think. When we feel something, like happiness or peace, are we not one with it? Can we be absent, or separated from a feeling? Of course not. Our task is to remember and accept that the only real feeling or emotion we have is Love. So, remember, if fear is felt, let it go. How do we let it go? Do we want to live in the feeling of fear? Does it feel good? Fear does its best to command us to abandon our natural home of Peace.

How do we let go of a feeling of fear that seems to cling to us and grab our attention? How do we let go? For me, what has helped is to remember that fear is an active denial of the Presence of God/Love on our part. We don't want to deny God any longer. Recall that only Love is real. That only Perfect Love Exists. Then, choose Love and Peace. Say, "I choose Love, I Choose

Peace." Say it softly within your heart. Feel the Truth of it. No matter what appears as a fearful picture or appearance, choose Love. Choose Peace. Say it. Choose to "go home" to Kansas. Tap the heels of your ruby slippers together and wake up from the dream of 'not Love.' Dorothy's shoes were red, the color of the symbolic heart. She metaphorically tapped into Love. She remembered she was dreaming. When she woke up in Kansas, she was surrounded by those who loved her. It was all just a bad dream.

I recall when the *Wizard of Oz* analogy came to me years ago. Spirit was trying to deepen my understanding and acceptance that the world is in fact a dream. I was inspired to continually keep the whole *Wizard of Oz* story in mind as I was shown that it is a very close approximation of how we fell into the dream. Shortly after I began having *Wizard of Oz* thoughts, I began seeing a short old man, what we now call a "little person," walking around the neighborhood I had just moved into in Tampa. I didn't think too much of it until a few weeks later there was a story in the newspaper that this man that I was seeing had actually played a part in the *Wizard of Oz* movie. He played the part of a Munchkin. Spirit was literally confirming the fact that the appearance world we seem to see is a dream and that we can choose to wake up and go home.

Lesson 169 By grace I live. By grace I am released.

Grace is the acceptance of the Love of God within a world of seeming hate and fear. By grace alone the hate

*and fear are gone, for grace presents a state so
opposite to everything the world contains, that those
whose minds are lighted by the gift of grace cannot
believe the world of fear is real.*

The acceptance of the Love of God within the dream of
hate and fear includes the acceptance that we were
created by the Love of God. Love can't but create Love.
Cats create kittens. Apple trees create apples. Cats
don't create puppies, nor do apple trees grow oranges
on their branches. Wine comes from grapes, and Love
comes from God. Acceptance of the Love of God
includes acceptance of our divine Holiness. Remember
always, there is no cruelty in God.

Remember our Holiness. You are Holy. You are the
creation of God. God is Perfect Holiness. So, pause
now. Pretend that God created you with a magic wand.
His wand would have been in the wardrobe where God
keeps all His creation stuff.

So Love opens His wardrobe and puts on His robe of
Light in preparation to create us. He then reaches back
into the wardrobe for His wand. But instead of finding
just His one perfect 'Love creation wand,' He finds a
second wand, one that He had never seen before. Both
wands have a label.

The first one He takes out is the only wand He has ever
used. It glows brightly with golden light. The label on it
says "You are Perfect Love and Peace, just as I am."

"I love this wand", says God with a smile, "I love creating something just like Me. So loving and happy and perfect, just like Me!"

Then God reaches in and takes out the second wand. It's kind of heavy and dark. No glow at all. God reads the label. It says, "You are Perfect Fear, unlike Me in every way."

God holds the two wands in his hands. "Let's see, I know only Perfect Love and Peace. I see the word "fear" on the other wand but have no clue what it means. I didn't create fear, whatever that is, so it is meaningless. I don't even know where this wand came from. Never seen it before in my life. Where did it come from? Then God remembered a couple of the Sons came to Him recently and asked something about wanting to be special and have a body to be special in. God remembers laughing at the idea as impossible. It then dawned on him that one of his rascal Sons slipped the fear wand into his wardrobe thinking maybe God wouldn't notice. God laughed again. "Sometimes my children are so silly." God then looked at the wand with a smile, and because the wand of fear was not created by God, it did not exist. With a wink of the eye of Truth, it disappeared.

Love then smiles to Himself, lifts the wand of Perfect Peace and Love, and in the sparkle of the moment, there we are. A spirit of Perfect Light, shining with the radiance and happiness of Love Itself. Our eyes of Light open and we greet our Creator with a smile. And our Creator sheds a tear of joy. So happy is He who can now share His eternal Love with Love. So Joyful is He who can now dance with Love. So bursting with Love is He Who now sees the Self of His Love as us.

You and I, the Love of His Spirit, burst forth with the same Loving essence as our Creator. Dancing with joy, singing with gratitude and happiness.

After a few moments in the realization of our creation, we sit with God to get to know Love a bit better. No words are spoken, but somewhere within us, we realize that we have the free will to accept our creation as Perfect Love in the exact Image of our Creator. Or, we are free to reject or deny our perfection. God watches our thoughts. To Him, it's an obvious choice, but He can't tell us what to do because we were created free. He hopes we make the choice to accept our Innocent Perfection, but he can't tell us what to do.

We look around and notice the One Wand of creation. If God has only one wand, there must be nothing but love, peace and happiness. In that very instant, we make the right choice. We accepted the "Word" of God spoken to us in our creation:

ACIM Lesson 276 The Word of God is given me to speak

What is the Word of God? "My Son is pure and Holy as Myself". And thus did God become the Father of the Son He loves, for thus he was created. This is the Word His Son did not create with Him, because in this His Son was born. Let us accept His Fatherhood and all is given us. Deny we were created in His Love and we deny our Self, to be unsure of Who we are, of Who our Father is and for what purpose we have come. And yet we need but acknowledge Him Who gave His Word to us in our creation, to remember Him and so recall our Self.

Because we all accepted the Love of God in our creation, we lived in the Garden of Eden, so to speak. The garden of having no needs. And yet God in His wisdom and His Love for His Children, knew that perhaps they would play with the idea of choice. God, being the God He Is, left nothing to chance, by not creating chance. God placed the One Wand within the hearts of His Creation, knowing that someday his children would seemingly leave on a journey from their awareness of their perfection and would need to find their way Home. The prodigal son would realize that he was dreaming a dream of leaving Home and would need to remember the Word in which he was created. That Word was within the One Wand of the Christ Light that God had placed within him. There would be difficult times within the dream of the forgetting of God and of forgetting our Holy Self. God could see that "the forgetting" would become a painful and lonely detour into the world of fear. God could see that we would yearn to find peace and happiness. God saw the dream

163

coming and left nothing to uncertainty and chance. Such is the Love of our Father.

God ordained that there would come a point in the dream wherein the darkness was to be no more. Jesus--Yeshua--our Brother of the Light, the Prince of Peace and the Guardian of God's Kingdom of Love, drew his first breath as a baby, and proceeded to steadfastly awaken us from the dream. The Wand of Christ lies deep within us all. Jesus remembered his Light and understood its message. The Wand of Light, the Holy Spirit of the Christ of each of us, is always there ready to reignite. The spark that reignites it is the call of Love within calling us to return Home to Peace, to the Garden of Eden. All that is needed is the *acceptance of the Love of God* within this dream of hate and fear. A deep-felt acceptance will re-light the Wand within. This is the sacred Light within each of us. This is the Holy Spirit. For the Wand within was God's answer to what we thought of as the concept of choice that was foreseen by God. We thought there may be a choice between the Perfect Peace of Love and something else. But when the dream becomes too painful to go on, the memory of the Love of our creation is triggered. And we will find, as we look within to the words inscribed on the One Wand of Christ Light, the words with which we were created:

You are Love. Perfect and Holy as I AM.

We then begin to remember, to awaken, realizing there never was a choice. Thank God there never was a real

164

choice. We were protected all along from ourselves. We were never in danger because we never left Heaven except in a bad dream. The Wand, the Sacred Light was there all along. The Truth was there all along. Never do we need to choose between fear and the Peace of Love. For there *is* only our perfect Love that we all share. Only Love and Peace and Holiness was placed within us. All else that we seem to see does not exist.

ACIM Lesson 230 Now I will seek and find the peace of God

In peace I was created. And in peace do I remain. It is not given me to change my Self. How merciful is God my Father, that when he created me he gave me peace forever. Now I ask to be but what I am. And can this be denied me, when it is forever true?

In *the* realization that we never left our Peace-Filled Home of Heaven, our eyes can begin to look to the Light to guide us back to the Awareness that only Truth of Peace and Holiness is True, and nothing else is true. We can open our eyes from the dream of death to the Truth of our creation of and as the Eternal Bliss of the Peace of Love. What is the Truth? Oneness.

The Truth is that it is impossible to not be as you were created by God:

ACIM lesson 110 I am as God created me.

*I am as God created me. Let us declare this truth as often as we can. This is the Word of God that sets you free. **This is the key that opens up the gate of Heaven**, and lets you enter in the Peace of God and His eternity.*

It is True that we cannot be different from Love. It is True that we, being Love, do not need to look across the water to an island of Love and wish we were on the Island of Love, all the while emphasizing the rough waters between our hell and the Truth. It is True that it is impossible not to be the Love we are. There is no gap between Love and what we are. Love has no need to "ask" for anything, because it lacks nothing.

In deep meditation recently, in answer to my longing to feel the deep stable, unshakable Eternal Peace, directly from our Source, I heard:

*"**There is no gap between What I Am and What I Am.**"*

These words are the Words of God that are shared in the Oneness we are with God. They are God's Words, yet they belong to us, given to us in our creation. Take them into meditation. They are your own words, spoken from your Christ Self. These words are the **Seamless Robe of Light** that you are.

ACIM Introduction xi

Sin is defined as "lack of love". Since love is all there is, sin in the sight of the Holy Spirit is a mistake to be corrected, rather than an evil to be punished. Our sense

166

of inadequacy, weakness and incompletion comes from the strong investment in the "scarcity principle" that governs the whole world of illusions. From that point of view, we seek in others what we feel is wanting in ourselves. We "love" another in order to get something ourselves. That, in fact, is what passes for love in the dream world. **There can be no greater mistake than that, for love is incapable of asking for anything.**

Love and guilt cannot coexist, and to accept one
is to deny the other.
– ACIM

14

THE MYTH OF GUILT AND SHAME

I REMEMBER MAKING my first Communion at Blessed Sacrament Catholic Church in Somerville New Jersey. I was about 8 years old and in the second grade. I vividly recall sitting in the parking lot beforehand with thoughts of being sinful swirling through my head. During this time in a Catholic child's life, one is taught how sinful and guilty one is. How we were somehow born in sin. We are taught that right from the get-go we are guilty and most assuredly not perfect. We are anything but perfect. Even before we seem to be born, sin has stained our souls and condemned us to a life of guilt and shame. I was born flawed and guilty. I was a "born sinner."

The clear message taught by the church at that time was "you are a guilty sinner." I was taught that all those minor little human mistakes we make were sins that needed to be confessed to a man in a confessional box.

We needed to be forgiven. We are so despicable and cursed that a man in a dark confessional box needed to remove our sin for us by giving us a punishment of saying, on our knees, 10 Hail Mary prayers.

When I left the dark confessional booth, I felt nothing but shame, nothing but "less than" good. I was apparently deeply flawed. I was created flawed by a god who I needed to be afraid of, especially after I die. I remember thinking, oh crap, what if I am mean to my friend on a Monday, but I fall off a cliff and die on Tuesday before I could get into the dark confessional box on Saturday? Would I go to hell? Or maybe I would live in "limbo" forever to be without the love of God. Banished into oblivion.

In spite of the fact that none of it made any sense to me, at some level on the surface, I accepted my flawed guilty self as what I must be. I mean, that was the drum beat of the Catholic Church and in fact, most Christian religions. Flawed sinner. Yup, just put your head down and accept the sad fact that you are not perfect and that accepting that fact may get you to heaven. Feel guilty, really guilty, especially because Jesus suffered and died for you.

As I sat in the parking lot of church before I was to make my first communion, I was going over the words that we were to speak during mass to "prepare" us to receive communion, which the church teaches is the actual body and blood of Jesus. The words we were taught, as Catholics throughout the world, are these:

169

"I am NOT WORTHY to receive you (referring to Jesus), but only say the word and I shall be healed".

In this ritual that is repeated a gazillion times throughout the world, we are continually misidentified as an "unworthy" creation of God. We are taught to drum this into our mind. The ego dream of death, this god of fear we are taught to worship, takes the place of the God of Love in our mind and heart, demanding our loyalty. And so, in fear, we go along with this preposterous message of sin and unworthiness, never getting to remember who we really are as the perfect creation of the Love of God.

In the parking lot, with these words in mind I heard another Voice. It said to me very clearly, **"You are perfect, not a sinner."**

The Voice was distinct and focused and certain. When I heard it, I recognized it, and the feeling of joy lit me up. I could actually feel a lifting up, a rise or a shift to a more peaceful place. I know now that it was the Voice of Truth, the Holy Spirit, the Spirit of God. In that parking lot of the church on the hill, I simply felt a wave of "release" pass through me and carry me to a place of smiling happy peace. I knew that what the Voice said was true. I just knew it. I knew that I was perfect, and for a moment or two it felt awesome!

But then as quickly as the feeling of truth came about, another voice jumped in and said, "You are wrong for even thinking that. You are so wrong. Who do you think you are to think that you are perfect and not a sinner?" This voice, the false ego little self, kept repeating the same thought over and over until it was able to block out the truth again from my mind. Even that being so, I never forgot what that loving voice said to me. That I was perfect, not a sinner. I didn't forget. But I did bury it. I was even afraid to share this thought with anyone in fear that I might be even more of a sinner for having entertained it as true. I kept it to myself, hoping it was really true despite that all of my world was telling me that there was something wrong with me.

Even the "Hail Mary" prayer that we are punished with has these words: **"Holy Mary Mother of God, pray for US SINNERS now and at the hour of our death. Amen"**

Yikes! There it is again; we are sinners.

What happens when we repeat something over and over and over again millions of times worldwide? We start to accept it. We believe it. And there is nothing that could be more spiritually deceptive than to accept and believe a lie about ourselves. Because then we begin to live in the darkness of the lie, instead of in the Light of the Love of God. When we can no longer seem to feel and know this Love, our hearts become dark and hopeless. We feel lost, and then we turn to the world to tell us who we are. The world is only too happy to tell us about ourselves. The world that I refer to, and the world that Jesus was speaking of when he told the parable of the prodigal son, was the dream world that appears to us and does its best to convince us that it is real. That we should believe it and accept what it tells us about ourselves. Remember, we did this to ourselves by choosing to believe the lies of the ego fear. By choosing Love as forgiveness, the fearful dream is undone, and we can remember we never did leave Heaven. We can wake up to Perfect Peace.

The world says we are weak, sinful, flawed and prey to sickness, injury, and poverty. And we believe it. What other choice have we had? We now have another choice. When life gets to the point of being so painful and miserable, we realize that what we have taught ourselves is a lie:

ACIM Chapter 2 III

"*Tolerance for pain may be high, but it is not without limit. Eventually everyone begins to recognize, however dimly, that there must be a better way. As this recognition becomes more firmly established, it becomes a turning point*"

Please understand something. By no means is religion devoid of teaching love. Most religions do teach about love. Unfortunately, most also teach of fear from the same pulpit. God and fear, Love and Fear, cannot occupy the same space, the same pulpit. Period.

Try to hold a thought of love and a thought of fear at the same time. You will see that you cannot. Try to hold the thought of love and hate at the same time. You cannot. Try to hold the thought of an earthquake and a peaceful mountain lake at the same time. You cannot. Try to hold the thought of a God of Love and a god of fear at the same time. You cannot.

One cannot feel hot water in the shower at the same time as feeling cold water in the same shower. It is one or the other. So what we do in the shower is move the handle to the middle of hot and cold. And we merely get warm. Not hot. Not cold. Just warm. And we happily settle for that. We compromise. A little hot, a little cold. Mix them together, and both are gone.

Mix the reality of love with the concept of hate or fear. What is left is nothing. This is the world of appearances. It's the world of nothingness pretending to be something. It is the "worldview" that is taught by many religions. Many. Not all. But far too many.

ACIM CHAPTER 27 III

"You have decided that your brother is a symbol (the image or picture of a body that we have substituted for our Real Brother of Perfect Bodiless Light) for a "hateful love" (most human relationships), a weakened power", and above all a "living death". And so he has no meaning to you, for he stands for what is meaningless. He represents a double thought, where half is cancelled out by the remaining half. Yet even this is quickly contradicted by the half it canceled out, and so they are both gone. And now he stands for nothing. Symbols (images, pictures and appearances) which but represent

ideas that cannot be must stand for empty space and nothingness. Yet nothingness and empty space cannot be interference. What can interfere with the Awareness of Reality (Truth/Heaven/Eternal Peace/Love) is the belief that there is something there."

Accepting into our minds any notion that one should in fact have a "healthy fear of God" and at the same time trying to accept God's love into our hearts is at best, confusing. To accept that the Reality or Truth of God can be *both* Love and fear is spiritually deceptive. Like combining hot and cold water in the shower and ending up with something in the middle, combining love and fear makes lukewarm spiritually. The attempt to combine or balance love and fear is the attempt to make both true. But only Truth is True, and nothing else exists. Only Love Is. And God Is Love. God Is. What can we say or think after the acceptance of God Is? We smile and go about our day, knowing that the memory of Truth, that Only God Is, is beginning to surface.

ACIM lesson 169. By grace I live. By grace I am released.

Oneness is simply the idea God is. And in His being, He encompasses all things. No mind holds anything but Him. We say, "God is", and then we cease to speak, for in that knowledge words are meaningless. There are no lips to speak them, and no part of mind sufficiently distinct to feel that it is now aware of something not itself. It has united with its Source. And like Source Itself, it merely is.

The point is that when we try to understand our dream world--the appearance world--through the lens of both love and fear, we remain confused and in chaos. In all of our relationships, especially what ACIM calls special love hate relationships, (husband wife, etc.) we attempt to balance love and hate/fear.

ACIM Chapter 16 IV

"Be not afraid to look upon the special hate relationship, for freedom lies in looking at it. It would be impossible not to know the meaning of love except for this. For the special love relationship in which the meaning of love is hidden, is undertaken solely to offset the hate, but not let it go. Your salvation will rise clearly before your eyes as you look on this. You cannot limit hate. The special love relationship will not offset it, but merely drive it underground and out of sight. It is ESSENTIAL to bring it into sight and to make no attempt to hide it. FOR IT IS THE ATTEMPT TO BALANCE HATE (fear) WITH LOVE THAT MAKES LOVE MEANINGLESS TO YOU. The extent of the SPLIT that lies in this (frustrating attempt) you do not realize. And until you do, the split (the "separation "from Love Only) will remain unrecognized and therefore unhealed."

When the world teaches us to integrate and accept both Love and fear as real, we remain confused and live and believe in this nothingness. This is the world of duality.

Happy and sad. Rich and poor. Male and female. Hot and cold. Each cancels the other out. We live in a dream of nothingness that ends and begins with the concept of death. You see, how can a body that begins to die the moment it appears to be born be called "life?" It is nothing but death masquerading as life. How can there be a "living death?"

It is time to wake from the dream of death, desolation and misery. It is time to return home to the awareness of the Kingdom of Heaven that exists right where we stand. Right where we appear to be. It's right here. No need to go find it "out there." There is a need to dissolve the blocks that we have to awareness of the Eternal Presence of the Kingdom of Love. Yes, there is that need. *A Course in Miracles* is the most powerful tool we have at our disposal. Its gifts remove the blocks to the memory of the Love of God that we have forgotten by denying it. By denying the Love of God, we have accepted the false emotion of fear as our god. But as the Course says, denial depends on our real belief in *what* is denied:

ACIM Chapter 11 III

Fear and love are the only emotions of which you are capable. One is false, for it was made out of denial, and denial depends on the real belief in what is denied for its own existence.

*By interpreting fear correctly **as a positive affirmation of the underlying belief it masks**, you are undermining*

*it's perceived usefulness by rendering it useless.
Defenses (to the Love of God as your Holy Self) which
do not work at all are **automatically discarded**. If you
raise what fear conceals to **clear-cut, unequivocal
predominance**, fear becomes meaningless. You have
denied its power to conceal love, which was its only
purpose. The mask you have drawn across the face of
love has disappeared.*

The Truth is that at one "time" we knew only God and
nothing else but God. We now have "Love Awareness
amnesia" induced by the hypnotic suggestion of the
false ego idea that there is something other than the
Love and Peace of God. Joel Goldsmith beautifully and
accurately describes the appearance world:

The New Horizon—from the "The Infinite Way"

*The sense which presents pictures of discord and
inharmony, disease and death, is the universal
mesmerism which produces the entire dream human
existence. It must be realized that the entire human
scene is mesmeric suggestion, and we must rise above
the desire for even good human conditions. Understand
fully that suggestion, belief, or hypnotism is the
substance or fabric, of the whole mortal universe and
that human conditions of both good and evil are dream
pictures having no reality or permanence.*

There is a cure for our denial of Love and the hypnotic
spell of fear we have fallen under. There is a treatment
plan. This treatment plan is the Plan of Light and

Forgiveness. It is what Jesus called the Plan of Atonement. It is the Plan to help us shake off the cobwebs from our minds, the mesmerism from our minds, and to remember who we are. It is the Plan to help us stop pretending that we are something other than perfect pure Innocence, Pure Holiness. The Plan is in place. We just need to trust the Present Love of God and nothing else. *A Course in Miracles* is the treatment plan. It's the prescription written by God, for what ails us. It is the treatment Plan to remove the pain of living in the thought that we are something other than as God created us. It is the antidote to the feeling of hopelessness, unhappiness, depression and struggle.

About 15 years ago, I was led by Spirit to Sedona Arizona. I was traveling with a group of friends that I had met over the years. For a 3- or 4-year period we would meet somewhere as dictated by spirit. One of the most important experiences that happened in Sedona was that I was given a prayer by one of my friends. She said Spirit inspired her that I was to go up into the red rocks of Sedona and that I was to read the prayer out loud, into the canyons below.

So early one morning we drove up into the red canyons. I walked a bit deeper amongst the red rocks and read this "prayer" aloud:

"The Great Invocation"

From the point of Light within the Mind of God,
Let Light stream forth into the minds of men,
Let Light descend on Earth,
From the point of Love within the Heart of God,
Let Love stream forth into the hearts of men,
May Christ return to Earth

From the center where the Will of God is known
Let purpose guide the little wills of men,
The purpose which the Masters know and serve,

From the center which we call the race of men,
Let the Plan of Love and Light workout,
And may it seal the door where evil dwells,

Let Light and Love and Power restore the Plan on
Earth.

Don't let the sound of your own wheels drive you crazy,
Lighten up while you still can, don't even try to understand,
Just find a place to make your stand and take it easy.

-Jackson Browne, Take It Easy

15

PRAYER OF LOVE

WHAT WAS IT THAT my visit with Gary had awakened in me? What was the gentle stirring that I felt? I was far from sure. But again, I knew it felt good, and it felt right. At some point later I came to realize that Gary's help was clearly Divinely orchestrated. Our meeting was part of the Plan of God's Salvation. The script, as the *Course* calls it, of the way home.

The sense of relief Gary gave me was on two levels. Or maybe really three levels. The first was simple friendship and kindness. Here was a man who didn't know me but went out of his way to help me. We laughed a lot. He was always upbeat, always encouraging and supportive. Always. Perhaps that was his greatest gift to me. A friend in the midst of a raging storm. It's just not possible to convey the impact that his friendship had on me. It changed my life and sent me in a spiritual direction. It was no accident that I came to know him.

Because of his unbelievable psychic gifts, he was also able to help me through the twists and turns of my divorce and starting a new life. At that time my mind was so filled with taking care of my two young daughters and difficult financial matters, Spirit's guidance, through Gary, relieved and calmed me many times throughout the divorce and life rebuilding process. Sometimes I just couldn't see clearly. But he always could.

It would be accurate to say that God, the God That Is Love, had scripted us to meet in the dream. The Plan. The script called for our meeting and friendship. We have known each other for centuries of dream lifetimes.

During this time, his career was blossoming. He was in demand on radio drive time talk shows in the Tampa Bay Area, and his reputation quickly spread throughout the United States. His calendar filled up with appointments and appearances. He had big name celebrity clients from Hollywood and around the country. In spite of his busy schedule, as Divinity would have it, he always took my calls or made quick arrangements to meet with me. In every sense, Gary was a gift from God, there to help steer me through a difficult period. The Holy Spirit made sure that when I needed help, He would make Gary available.

One example of many, late one afternoon, towards the end of my divorce process, I needed to talk to him about something having to do with custody of my daughters. I was on my way to a Rays baseball game in St Petersburg with my two daughters. At that time, Gary had moved to Atlanta to do radio in a bigger market. Needing to talk to him, I called his cell phone and left a message for him to call me. I had not heard back from him by the time we arrived at the stadium and found our seats, which were not together. My daughters had seats at ground level, first base side. My seat was the next level up, approximately 20 rows behind them. I still had not heard from Gary but figured I would later sometime. At the seventh inning stretch, my daughters walked up towards where I was sitting.

And right in back of my daughters, there was Gary walking three feet behind them! I could not believe what I was seeing. He had moved to Atlanta. How in the world did he end up sitting and then walking right behind my daughters at a professional baseball game in St. Petersburg? How was this possible?

He then walked right up to me with a smile, and in his North Carolina accent said, "Hey Paul, how are you?" He explained that he didn't even know why he was at the game. He was just back in town visiting a friend and God told him to go to the game. I could not believe it! I was just dumbfounded. After I recovered from the shock, he and I went back to the ramp area and discussed the issue I was concerned about. After he relieved my worry, there again came a deep sense of peace. Gary kept encouraging me not to quit in my efforts to get custody of my daughters. He "saw" that in the end I would be successful, which turned out to be true. I did get custody, and it made all the difference. Gary's encouragement and spiritual insights were instrumental in my resolve to not give up. In a sense, Gary was very much like the embodiment of a Guardian Angel, literally walking behind my children up the stadium steps, guiding them to their dad.

Another time, after Gary had moved to Hollywood, Michelle and I took a weekend trip to New Orleans. Michelle wanted to stay in one of those boutique old hotels in the French Quarter. When we arrived, it smelled like cigarettes and felt dark. So we left and found a room on Canal Street, I believe it was the Sheraton. After arriving there, Gary called me just to catch up. He asked what I was doing. I told him I was in New Orleans for the weekend. I asked him what he was doing. He said he was in New Orleans for the weekend. Really, you're kidding! I asked him where he was staying. He said he was staying at the Sheraton on Canal Street. Really. Me, too. He was just a few floors above us.

I could tell many more stories like this. The point is that miracles are available to us on this journey home. I know I am here to be helpful and that I have done my best to continually choose the Power of Peace and the guidance of the Holy spirit. It is clear that God has provided earthly guidance to me to make sure that my path is clear. Perhaps it is that I came into this world with a mission still yet not fully known to me. So be it. There is no will but the Will, the Love of God.

The third level of Gary's help was the spiritual level. I suppose really it was the first level, or reason for our meeting. Yet, because of his remarkable friendship and psychic ability to calm the storms in my life, I was much more open spiritually. Soon, although not soon enough, I came to the realization that my personal life circumstances were part of the Plan of God, through the Holy Spirit, to open me up, to crack me open. With this cracking open of my belief system, I opened up--or awakened to-- a world that I never knew existed. That "new" world that was opening up to me, or more accurately, the world that I was willing to open up to, was Spirit, the Kingdom of Love, the Presence of God's Love as the only Reality.

This opening up has been a slow process. For some, awakening occurs in what seems to be a nanosecond. Like Eckhart Tolle. Perhaps Paul of the Bible also had one of those nanosecond awakenings where in one moment there is the darkness that we experience, and then in the next moment, there is only Light and Peace, and the darkness of the world of fear is gone forever.

But my process of awakening to the Truth, like the vast majority of people looking to find the way Home to Peace, has been a slow chipping away, or undoing of the seeming miserable appearance world. Very much like Michael Angelo who saw the sculpture within the block of raw marble. The truth is in us, buried and out of physical sight. Very much there, here, within us. In the Holy Spirit's Vision, or Way of looking or perceiving, we can see God's finished work of art that we really are. This Christ Vision, or "way of seeing," is merely our natural sight that has been veiled or blocked by our decision to look upon guilt. It was, and continues to be, a decision. This decision, though, can be changed. We can decide differently. This power to decide is really the only power we have in the dream:

ACIM Text Chapter 14 III The Decision for Guiltlessness

Each day, each hour and minute, even each second, you are deciding between the crucifixion and the resurrection; between the ego and the Holy Spirit. The ego is the choice for guilt; the Holy Spirit is the choice for guiltlessness. The power of decision is all that is yours. What you decide between is fixed, because there are no alternatives except truth and illusion. And there is no overlap between them, because they are opposites that cannot be reconciled, and cannot both be true. You are guilty or guiltless, bound or free, unhappy or happy.

Jesus is impressing upon us in this moment, that understanding and *accepting* the fact that the dream we see was and is a decision that we made, is *crucial* to the healing of our mind. He wants us to understand that the same decision-making power that denied the Light and

Innocence of Heaven is the same power that can now decide to deny our denial of God, of Light, of Innocence.

This understanding is key. Because if we don't open our eyes to this fact, we will continue to flounder in misery within the dream of death, chasing our own tails. Escape back into the state of Heaven will elude us. The escape from the dream of judgment and guilt and never-ending problems that we dream of can only be accomplished by the discipline of gentle persistence and gentle insistence that we remember the Truth. To remember only our Christ Mind, "where" we really abide. Even now, that is "where" we abide. It is the Garden of Eden.

Gary Spivey was a gentle messenger of God, there to catch me and initiate the memory my Christ Mind. Now, twenty years later, I can clearly see the Love of God at work. I have come to understand God and Spirit much differently, or in a new light than I was taught by the world. Gary was a messenger who was there to gently crack open the door. Then, my mind opened to the acceptance of the Truth in *A Course in Miracles*. Although Gary helped initiate my opening to Spirit, the "work" was mine to do.

Please keep in mind that if we ask for help from Spirit, a "Gary Spivey" will be sent to help. My initial asking for help was unspoken. It was the asking of my heart to return home to peace. Those of you who have felt the longing for peace will be led to the right teachers and mentors. In fact, over the years, as one teacher of mine has completed his or her time with me, another arrived to continue the process of helping me to decide, on a deeper and deeper level, to heal my mind of the denial of the Love and Light of God. There were several in my life after Gary. The key at the beginning of the journey is to accept and recognize that on some level, you asked for help at a point in your dream where it became too painful to continue to fool yourself that the world of appearances, conjured up by the ego thought of fear, was real.

The pivotal time in the dream of suffering for most of us is when we reach the point where we can no longer control the dream. Something has happened that we may not have expected. We are deeply disillusioned by an event, circumstance or relationship. Financial issues, loss of job, divorce or sickness. We usually try and try to fix what's wrong. We try to work really hard at it, whatever the 'it' is. And it doesn't work. All our work and human effort doesn't fix it. Despite all that we've been taught about how to control the world with education, hard work and attention to detail, somehow our world stops working.

One of the first stops on the spiritual train to fix our broken world is "manifesting." This is the notion that when we want something to happen, we can hold a vision of it, and eventually "it" happens or "manifests." Please don't be fooled by this notion. I was for a while. I read all the manifesting vision board books and methods. Sometimes it even seems to work a little. But don't get caught in the ego trap of placing your "awareness" deeper into the world of appearance and images.

Trying to manifest is like going to the movies and attempting to change the movie that is already over, in the sense that is has been filmed and is in the "can." We can't sit in a theater and attempt to change the kind of car the main character drives or who she falls in love with. The script is written. It is what it is. But we can forgive it or overlook it as not real.

ACIM Lesson 158

*Time is a trick, a slight of hand, a vast illusion in which figures come and go as if by magic. Yet there is a plan behind appearances that does not change. **The script is written**. When experience will come to end your doubting has been set. For we but <u>see</u> the journey from the point at which it ended, looking back on it, imagining we make it once again: reviewing mentally what has gone by.*

The notion of manifesting is not much different than the traditional notion of praying to God to please make something happen. A prayer of supplication is the same idea as manifesting. They don't work. If these ideas worked, the dream world would not be the nightmare that it is. Why would a loving creator place us in a world of problem after problem and then have us pray to him to fix the problems? This creator places us in a world of disease and sickness, and then we pray to be cured. This creator places us in a world of limited resources over which we wage world wars, and then we pray for our soldiers and pray to win the war.

Bottom line is that we have accepted the lie that God kicked us out of the heaven of peace into a world of chaos and misery and then encourages us to pray to please stop being mean to us with all this fear and misery and death. "I will be good. I know I am a miserable sinner. But dear God, if you have it your heart, please cure my son's disease that you apparently exposed him to. Please don't take him from us. Take me instead⋯. etc."

We must reject this notion of God and His Plan.

When something our life goes "wrong," our minds spin out various ways to "fix" what went wrong. The "what went wrong" can be a financial matter, job loss, relationship issue or a health problem. If we are a person of traditional religious views, we pray to our concept of God to fix the "what went or is going wrong." We ask for intervention from a power beyond the concept of our human self to fix it, please. We ask for something outside of ourselves to consider our plight and misery and to change the what went wrong into something going right.

 No need for me to again explain why it makes no sense, other than to point out that we have been fooled into praying this way for centuries, and nothing in this world of appearances has changed. Nothing? Yes, nothing.

Three thousand years ago the people prayed to the gods of rain and sun and wind. Nothing happened. Each generation, the people in the dream have prayed to fix or change something that has gone wrong, a circumstance or event or a situation that is full of conflict and fear and uncertainty. Each and every generation for all of dreamtime has asked a power that is outside of sight to fix something on the "screen" of the dream.

Here is a bit of the lawyer in me. Where is the evidence that would prove that for thousands of years, this method of asking God to fix or give us something, works? There is none. Sure, there is a story here and there that something miraculous happens. Jesus would tell us it's part of the dream to keep us captured within the lie that we are separate from God. It's very much like when there is an outpouring of prayer in a city children's hospital. There are 50 families praying that their child be spared. But God only grants one wish per hospital per day. So, 1 child is cured by God and 49 children are ignored.

Understand what I am saying. There is a form of prayer that works. But "prayer" and "works" must be understood. For "works" is only seen in the results of the desire of the Heart within each of us. Traditional prayer is the deep desire to see something happen on the screen of the appearance world.

True prayer is the *releasing* of what we want to see or the way we desire that things should be, in favor of the desire to feel the Love and Peace of God within one's self. It is the desire of the Son/Child for the Father only, releasing all else to Trust. True prayer then, is asking for, and therefore results in, the awareness of the Kingdom of Heaven, trusting, trusting, trusting that all else will be provided, even within the dream, for our highest good. True prayer is *" Thy Will be done."*

True prayer is the relinquishing, or letting go, of what it is that we think would bring us joy, happiness and peace. Now understand this. Understand what is being conveyed here. Slow down and take this in.

A Course in Miracles says that Prayer is the greatest gift that God gave to us or imparted within our very essence. This is the very base, or foundation of our "real power." In the **Supplement to A Course in Miracles Pamphlet, The Song of Prayer**, Jesus tells us···.

Prayer is the greatest gift with which God blessed His Son at his creation. It was then what it is to become; the single voice Creator and creation share; the song the Son sings to his Father, who returns the thanks it offers Him unto the Son. Endless the harmony and endless too the joyous concord of the Love they give forever to Each other.

Prayer is a way offered by the Holy Spirit to reach God. It is not merely a question or entreaty. It cannot succeed until you realize it asks for nothing. How else

191

could it serve its purpose? It is impossible to pray for idols and hope to reach God. True prayer must avoid the pitfall of asking to entreat. Ask, rather, to receive what is already given; to accept what is already there.

Stop here for a second. Jesus wants us to take this in. Think for a moment. How many of us would give everything we have, everything we appear to own, travel across the globe and spend our last dollar, if we could just sit for a few minutes with Jesus. Really sit with him for a few minutes and talk about the things that are bothering us and causing us to feel not-peace, the feeling of anxiety and worry. We would go to any length to sit with him even for just a short while, because we know he has the answers for us.

What Jesus tells us *In A Course in Miracles, The Song of Prayer Pamphlet,* should cause a reaction within us to stop our own thinking. When he **tells** me something, I do my very best to slow down and listen. Just stop and listen to the soul who showed us the concept of death is a concept that he overcame and that we can overcome, if we just listen. We need just get over little ego personal selves and listen to him, as he continues and **tells** us:

To you who are in time a little while, prayer takes the form that best will suit your need. YOU HAVE BUT ONE. (one need). What God created one must recognize its oneness, and rejoice that what illusions seemed to separate is one forever in the Mind of God.

Prayer must now be the means by which God's Son leaves separate goals and separate interests by (behind) and turns his holy gladness to the truth of union in his Father and in himself.

Jesus continues to tell us:

Lay down your dreams (your goals and all the stuff you think you need that come with the dream), you holy Son of God, and rising up as God created you, dispense with idols and remember Him.

Prayer will sustain you now and bless you as you lift your heart up to Him in rising song that reaches higher and higher still, until both high and low have disappeared. Faith in your goal will grow and hold you up as you ascend the shining stairway to the lawns of Heaven and the gate of Peace. For THIS is prayer, and here salvation is.
This is the Way.
It is God's Gift to you.

Beautiful.

 Jesus is **telling** us, reminding us of something that we once knew. That is, Jesus is telling us we have this power of prayer within us. It is our essence. But true prayer is not what we, in the dream, have come to understand as prayer. Jesus and the Holy Spirit are teaching us. They are not teaching new information. They are teaching us to remember. *A Course in*

Miracles is a beautiful book full of thousands of words designed to jog our memory of who we really are. That being the case, we are being encouraged to remember real prayer. We are being encouraged that we do not need to pray for specific things within the dream. We are to seek the Kingdom of Heaven by letting go of the seeking or asking for the stuff of dreams, in favor of desiring the Peace of God above all else. For you see, the Peace of God, which is characterized by Joy, is the Kingdom of Heaven. Sitting in true prayer really means just the deep quiet desire for nothing but the desire to feel, the be aware of, the warmth and safety of Heaven. Nothing else. Just that. The Presence of God, which is characterized by deep peace, the absence of anxiety brought on by human thoughts.

I am repeating this here for a reason. There are certain ideas or concepts that are so important to our freedom, to our salvation, that they will be repeated. Jesus gave me a way of helping this idea of true prayer jell within me. It was key for me to understand the nature of this true prayer, but it wasn't sinking in, it wasn't really jelling until recently. Follow me here.

Let's take a very common issue in our lives that almost no one is exempted from. Scarcity of money. For those of you who have trust funds, there are likely issues of health and relationships. But this example right now is about money to pay the bills. Money to pay the rent and keep the electricity on for yourself and for your family.

Typical prayer, in my experience, would be the sitting or kneeling, and the asking of God, the Santa Claus-like man in the invisible world somewhere to please, please bring me money to pay the rent or mortgage. To me, this form of prayer has always seemed logical in light of what I had been taught by the world. It was logical because I was taught that God had all the power, and he loved me. (even though he allegedly created a hell for me to burn in if I committed too many or certain kinds of sin.) But with that general background of my knowledge about this God, I figured He loves me, or at least likes me. And I was a generally a good person, trying my best to help those around me and to be kind. So, if I ask him for something, like mortgage money to appear in my bank account, or at least in the form of plenty of business, he would have no reason not to grant my prayer. Right? I mean, I don't run drugs or kill people. Most of us don't. So why would God deny our request to fix the issues of in our world? Paying our rent or mortgage is kind of important, even though it's a dream. We can't tell the landlord or the bank that it is a dream, so no need to pay you. Not happening.

Here again, Holy Spirit is whispering in my ear to remind us, through these words on this page, but more so through the words in *A Course in Miracles,* that we are praying all day long. Each second of every day that we seem to experience, we are praying, we are asking. Jesus is reminding right now to stop thinking of prayer as something reserved for sitting in a church pew, or the lighting of a church candle or the sitting at home asking God to give us something.

We pray all day long by the *feeling* that we hold within. Our all-day asking, our all-day prayer is the asking for Peace or the asking for fear. Period. Jesus said PERIOD. Prayer is a feeling, a deep quiet feeling of peace above all else. The feeling of being not apart from Warm Radiant Joy that Is God. The Kingdom of Heaven. The feeling of not being away from the Kingdom, rather it is the feeling of being the Kingdom Itself. So, we pray all day by the feeling and the belief we hold about "the whereabouts" of God. We truly "pray" when we connect with the feeling that "I and the Father, the Kingdom of Heaven, are One. "

Or is our all-day prayer the choice to feel we are alone and at the mercy of the world, fighting our way through? That being the case, we are *asking* to be shown that we are at the mercy of the world and that we are alone, and we need to fight our way through it. This way of praying is really the asking to be separate from the Kingdom of Perfect Peace. Here's why.

I am picking up here on what helped the jelling of the understanding of true prayer for me.
When we don't have the money for the mortgage that's due in 10 days, we begin to panic. Let's say we are working but having a bad month at our self-employment, or maybe we had emergency unexpected expenses for the tenth time this year. We are in anxiety and worry. We are anything but deeply peaceful. We are on edge and swirling with "what if" thoughts. What if we

can't pay it on time? What if we get kicked out? Where will we live? And on and on and on.

Let's say on top of not having enough money, we also have a significant health issue. In addition to that, your child is having problems keeping up grades in high school, jeopardizing college scholarship chances, and on top of that your car broke down right after the warranty ran out. Holy smokes! What do I pray for first?? Into prayer we go. We sit at the kitchen table or on a park bench or in a church pew, and we begin with our list of the things that are threatening us and causing us fear and anxiety.

Jesus tells us that true prayer is not the words that we use, but the feeling in our heart, in our being. He tells us that the prayer of our heart, the asking of our heart, is granted. So, what is in our heart? The human heart is a symbol of feeling and distribution of life blood. When we want to convey love in a text message, we might place a heart emoji at the end. So, the prayer is really the emotion of our heart. The physical heart pumps blood with oxygen and nutrients all throughout our body keeping it "alive." The human heart sends messages to the organs in the blood it pumps, telling the organs to keep functioning. In a sense, the human heart is praying, or asking or even instructing the body through the blood it pumps out.

Now, what does our spiritual heart pray for? If the spiritual heart, or the "within-ness" that we feel, is not at peace, then we are praying for "not peace." And when we pray for situations that we are worried and anxious about; we cannot be at peace. It's just not possible to pray to fix a scary situation and be at peace. Peace and not peace cannot be in the same place at the same time. Heaven and hell cannot occupy the same space. A prayer for something I need and don't have, *is* a feeling of not peace. Asking for something specific in the dream is like asking God to prolong our agony in the dream. In effect, we are saying to God, "Look, God, I know I left the Kingdom of Heaven to make my own illusory miserable world, but I ran out of money, and I need you to make some appear for me here in the dream. I need you to make my dream better. I have a lot of anxiety about not being able to pay my bills. Yes, yes, I know I have everything in my true state of peace, but right now I need to make my dream better so that I can get more deeply lost in it. Ok? Do we have a deal?"

We are actually begging God to make us more miserable. Or actually, on a more profoundly deeper level, we are asking––or praying––to ourselves to keep ourselves in the state of anxiety. Peace is what we are. True prayer is the asking for the Peace of God above else. It is the seeking of the Kingdom Heaven the effect of which is that all else needed will be provided. This is my favorite lesson of prayer:

ACIM Lesson 185 I want the peace of God.

To say these words is nothing. But to mean these words is everything. If you could just mean them for just an instant, there would be no further sorrow possible for you in any form; in any place or time. Heaven would be completely given back to full awareness, memory of God entirely restored, the resurrection of all creation fully recognized.

No one can mean these words and not be healed. He cannot play with dreams, nor think he is himself a dream. He cannot make a hell and think it real. He wants the peace of God, and it is given him. For that is all he wants, and that is all he will receive. Many have said these words. But few indeed have meant them. You have but to look upon the world you see around you to be sure of how very few there are. The world would be completely changed, should any two agree these words express the only thing they want.

And also:

ACIM Chapter 10 III

When a brother is sick it is because he is not asking for peace, and therefore does not know he has it. The acceptance of peace is the denial of illusion, and sickness is an illusion.

As we are created in the image of God, our true prayer then is to simply ask to remember who we are and then be led by Christ in all matters. Asking for things to be added to the dream is asking God to be Who He is not. Gratitude for the eternal gifts of the Peace of the Love of God is our prayer. **"Thank you, God, for taking care of my day"** is a powerful, peaceful prayer.

ACIM Lesson 185 Love is the way I walk in gratitude

*Today we learn to think of gratitude in place of anger,
malice and revenge. We have been given everything. If
we refuse to recognize it, we are not entitled therefore
to our bitterness, and to a self-perception which
regards us in a place of merciless pursuit, where we are
badgered ceaselessly, and pushed about without a
thought of care for us or for our future. Gratitude
becomes the single thought we substitute for these
insane perceptions. God has cared for us and calls us
Son. Can there be more than this?*

 In the state of heaven there is no gap in which there
could be an unfulfilled need. There is no gap in our
Christ vision. In it, we see only what God created.
Holiness and Peace is all that will register to our Christ
Mind when we 'look' only with Christ vision, which is
the forgiving of the appearance world. It is looking past
the forms to the Light beyond the form. And when we
look past the form to the Holy Light that is there, we
are safe. We are in God's Hands. We are home in this
Light.

When most of us go to work or begin a project, with few
exceptions, there is a lag time between when we
actually do the work, see the results and get paid. We
generally have to do something in the world and then at
some point later we receive a benefit or paycheck. The
bottom line is that the false appearance world that we

live in has trained our human perception, our human mind, to accept that there is a delay between the asking for something and the getting of that something.

Even when we pray in the traditional way to the traditional God, we, at best, expect a time delay between the prayer and the receiving. For instance, if we sit in a church and pray for rent money, we do not expect to walk out of church and find a stack of dollar bills on the front steps waiting for us. Well, you might laugh at that example as being too extreme and completely "unrealistic." You might say no, I don't expect a stack of dollars on the church steps, but I trust that God and His Angels will line everything up somehow, someway, so that my rent gets paid.

But even here again, there is a delay or a gap between a perceived need that we may have and the fulfillment of that need.

And in that "gap" or "delay" of an unmet need, there is fear and anxiety. We look with our human senses, which by their very false nature, feed us fear. We look at the checkbook and don't see numbers that are high enough to pay the bills. Or we look at other numbers on the blood test that are either too high or too low. Our senses then throw us into the cold sweat of fear. This is not peace. Our physical senses are pulling us out of peace. It's the way the ego stays relevant. But our natural inheritance of seeing with our natural Christ vision delivers a message to us of only peace:

ACIM lesson 159 I give the miracles I have received.

Christ's vision is the miracle in which all miracles are born. It is their source, remaining with each miracle you give, and yet remaining yours. It is the bond by which the giver and receiver are united in extension here on earth, as they are one in Heaven. Christ beholds no sin in anyone. And in His sight the sinless are as one. Their holiness was given by His Father and Himself.

Christ's vision is the bridge between the worlds. And in its power can you safely trust to carry you from this world into one made holy by forgiveness. Things which seem quite solid here are merely shadows there; transparent, faintly seen, at times forgot, and never able to obscure the light that shines beyond them. Holiness has been restored to vision, and the blind can see.

This (Christ's vision) is the Holy Spirit's single gift, the treasure house to which you can appeal with perfect certainty for all the things that can contribute to your happiness. All are laid here already. All can be received but for the asking. Here the door is never locked, and no one is denied his least request or his most urgent need. There is no sickness not already healed, no lack unsatisfied, no need unmet in this golden treasury of Christ.

What is it really that we are praying for when we ask for rent money or the healing of a sickness? We are really asking for peace. Because when the rent gets paid or the illness goes away, there is a feeling of the absence of "need." **And the absence of need is peace**. But in this appearance world of not–peace, not–God, after a few days, if not sooner, we realize the rent has to be paid again at the end of the next month, and now we have a new pain in our hip. Hello anxiety! Hello fear! Hello not-peace! Where have you been? I missed you! I have had 5 or 6 days without you, and I missed you! Let's do this dance of anxiety and fear and not-peace again! How am I going to pay that electric bill? And I have a pain in my stomach that won't go away. The pain in my leg went away, but now my stomach hurts. What if it is cancer? I don't have any insurance; what will I do? I know, I will pray to God and ask Him nicely if he will kindly pay the electric bill and cure my cancer. I bet if I am really passionate, he will cure me. Or better yet, ten Hail Marys. We all know Mary is who you ask to help you as a last resort. Like the football term for at the end of a game when there are 3 seconds on the clock. The quarterback tosses an 80-yard pass deep into the end zone on a hope and a prayer that somehow an offensive player catches it in a crowd of players, for a touchdown. That's a Hail Mary Pass.

What if we have been praying, praying, praying to God and He didn't cure 'it.' Well, then we go to Mary and maybe ask her to talk to God to let Him know how serious this is and to please reconsider curing it. You know "men" like God, they don't have the same compassion as, say, a woman like Mary. Or, if that doesn't work, you could ask Mary to talk Jesus into performing a miracle cure. Mary is good at that. Remember that wedding in Cana? It apparently was a great big wedding with lots of guests and dancing and drinking. But then they ran out of wine. It seems that

Mary was probably related to the wedding party because according to all biblical accounts, she was concerned that there was no more wine. Or maybe she just wanted another few glasses for her and Joseph. After all, they didn't get out much and she was happy to be out of the house. In any case, whatever her motivation, she really wanted more wine for the party. So, she asked Jesus to turn water into wine. I have no doubt that Jesus was more than capable of doing that. But, how did Mary know that? Was Jesus turning water into wine in the Joseph and Mary home? Since Mary is in the position of being able to tell Jesus which miracles to perform, she seems to be a safe bet to pray to when you really need something done. Moms don't hold back on telling their sons what to do. Just pray to Mary. She'll tell Jesus in a split second what to do.

The way we are taught to pray in this dream of not-peace is exactly as ridiculous as it sounds.
We are taught to pray within the dream, by ego, the false, imposter self, in order to instill in us on a deeper and deeper level that we are powerless and at the mercy of the dream events. The ego convinces us we are actually a figure in the dream. We are taught we should work hard and struggle to change and cure the problems of the world dream. We have been hoodwinked, *by our own choice*, into believing that we must work and struggle in this world to "make it a better place for our children." Really? How long have we been using that, on some level, as our motivation for acting like there is a "realness" in this world? You know how long? Thousands and thousands and thousands of

years. Kings and Queens, dynasties and regimes, investment bankers and Wallstreet all indulge us in the lie of preserving the world as being a worthwhile investment.

ACIM Chapter 12 III The Investment in Reality

I once asked you to sell all you have and give to the poor and follow me. This is what I meant: If you have no investment in anything in this world, you can teach the poor where their treasure is. The poor are merely those who have invested wrongly, and they are poor indeed! Because they are in need it is given you to help them. Consider how perfectly your lesson would be learned if you were unwilling to share their poverty. **For poverty is lack, and there is but one lack since there is but one need. (to remember we are one with, and therefore ARE, the Love of God).**

The world of appearances is the temptation to get us to pray for more and better appearances. More money, more health and better relationships because the lack thereof is keeping us awake at night. Do we bite the apple of appearance? *Or do we choose Peace?* For choosing to pray for something in the world appearance is asking God for a weapon to temporarily conquer a fear or solve a problem. I say temporarily because as soon as one problem in our world is solved, there is always another sneaking up behind us.

A prayer for anything other than the Peace of God is a prayer to be something other than the Son of God, the

Christ you are. A prayer for anything other than the Peace of God is an asking to leave and forget the Kingdom of Heaven. And remember, we pray all day in each and every moment. Pray to remember that YOU are Christ. Pray for the Peace of God above all else. Pray to remember you have been given everything.

We pray for the Peace of God, or we pray all our days for the appearance world of chaos to appear in a better way. Rest assured, that when we seek or pray for the Peace of God, letting go of all else, any all else that we need for our journey in this world will be provided. Pray, above all else, **"I want the peace of God." (lesson 185)**

Really mean it with all your heart and soul and mind. And trust that what is needed in form, will be provided without your asking. Trust also that if you needed "it," you would have "it." The focus now becomes the awareness of the Kingdom spread out before us. As we stay in the awareness, or in the "prayer" for Peace, our mind becomes re-aligned with the Will of God. The Will of God is the perfect, undisturbed eternal peace and happiness for his beloved Children.

Your trials did not come to punish you, but to awaken you.
-Paramahansa Yogananda

16

IN DIVINE ORDER

ONE OF THE MOST DIFFICULT challenges of the dreamworld life we seem to live is the many appearances in our personal lives of events, circumstances and people that don't make us happy. This feeling of not satisfied with a person's behavior or with an outcome causes us to react in a thought that says, in one way or another, "it shouldn't be like this, he shouldn't act like that or this should not have turned out this way." The voice or thought that says this is the ego thought. Remember, the ego is NOT you and the ego's job is to never be satisfied. The ego voice has a vested interest in making sure that we remain unsatisfied with everything in our world. The ego voice, which is NOT us, is the opinionated judger of all events and people. It is the voice that we have allowed in that discriminates, criticizes and critiques. It is the voice that pretends to be us and that we have chosen to identify with.

Here is a simplistic example. You are sitting in an outdoor café having lunch with your friend in the dream world we think of as our life. As your friend is filling you in on the latest gossip about one of the mothers at school, a woman walks by. Even though you don't know her, a voice in your mind begins to speak. It says, "I love her shoes, but I hate the yellow dress. I would never have worn that dress with those shoes. Her hair is ok, but it needs to be a little lighter." Then on and on the ego goes. This ego mind voice never shuts up, and it is the voice that we have come to believe is us. We believe it *is* us. When we hear it critiquing, we think it is us critiquing and judging and expressing opinions. We come to believe that the "who" I am doesn't like the yellow dress. The who I am has so many likes, dislikes, grievances, fears and loves. This voice that is pretending to be the "who I am" has become our guide and authority. This is what is meant by "identifying" with it. It 'masquerades' as the real us. We become identified *as* it. We listen to it even though, unknown to us, its main job is to keep us in fear and confusion and separate us from peace. We know this voice as the voice that comes across our mind and speaks of grievances, complaints, unfairness and threats to our safety and surety. It loves to bring threats to our attention to keep us off balance which produces anxiety and fear. It, in effect, brainwashes us into believing its voice and thoughts are ours.

It is very much like a person who is kidnapped and kept in captivity for a long period of time and begins to identify with the kidnapper. This is exactly what the ego voice has done to us. It first kills the Christ and then subtly gets us to identify with it as us.

This voice, which is NOT the voice of Love, warns us that danger is around every corner, and disaster is about to strike. Again, its chief weapon is threat. Its job is to keep us in a state of anxiety and uncertainty. Its job is to keep us in fear and grievances so that we can never rest in the Peace of God. The ego of the personal self is a voice that endlessly tortures us with what seems like logical fears and life complaints but are really designed to keep us in anxiety. The torture is like the sleep deprivation torture used by the military to provoke false confessions. The voice is continuous and loud. Its job is to wear us out to the point that it becomes easier to believe it is us.

The false ego voice essentially tells us that nothing is ever the way it should be, and nobody is acting like they should act. It then gets us to pray for things to change and be different than they are. The ego wants us to listen. The ego wants us to believe its grievances and complaints.

ACIM Lesson 68 Love holds no grievances

You who were created by Love like itself can hold no grievances and know your Self. To hold a grievance is to forget who you are. To hold a grievance is to see yourself as a body. To hold a grievance is to let the ego rule the mind and condemn the body to death. Perhaps you do not yet fully realize just what holding grievances does to your mind. It seems to split you off from your Source (Love) and make you unlike Him. It makes you believe that He is like what you have become, for no one can conceive of his Creator as unlike himself.

And:

ACIM Lesson 71 Only God's plan for salvation will work.

The ego's plan for salvation centers around holding grievances. It maintains that if someone else spoke or acted differently, if some external circumstance or event were changed, you would be saved. Thus, the source of salvation (peace) is constantly perceived as outside of yourself. Each grievance that you hold is a declaration, and an assertion in which you believe, that says, "If this were different, I would be saved." The change of mind necessary for salvation is thus demanded of everyone and everything except yourself.

The role assigned to your own mind in this plan, then, is simply to determine what, other than itself, must change if you are to be saved. According to this insane plan, any perceived source of salvation is acceptable provided it will not work. This ensures that the fruitless search will continue, for the illusion persists that, although this hope has always failed, there is still grounds for hope in other places and other things. Another person will yet serve better; another situation will yet offer success.

Such is the ego's plan for salvation. Surely you can see how it is in strict accord with the ego's basic doctrine, "Seek but do not find". For what could more surely guarantee that you will not find salvation than to channelize all your efforts in searching for where it is not.

And:

ACIM Lesson 73 I will there be light.

Idle wishes and grievances are partners or co-makers in picturing the world you see. The wishes of the ego gave rise to it, and the ego's need for grievances, which are necessary to maintain it, peoples it with figures that seem to attack you and call for righteous judgment. These figures become the middlemen the ego employs to traffic in grievances. They stand between your awareness and your brother's reality. Beholding them, you do not know your brother or yourself.

And:

ACIM Lesson 78. Let miracles replace all grievances.

Perhaps it is not quite clear to you that each decision that you make is between a grievance and a miracle. Each grievance stands like a dark shield of hate before the miracle it would conceal. And as you raise it up before your eyes, you will not see the miracle beyond. Yet all the while it waits for you in light, but you behold your grievances instead.

It is very helpful to be aware of what is going through our minds as we are about to pray. What's in our mind? What is in our heart? No matter the circumstance, no matter who we are, no matter what the subject, the theme is always the same. The theme of the prayer is never ever different.

The theme of the desire contained within the ego prayer is this:

Dear God, things are not right, and I want them to be different. I want my significant other to act differently towards me and my children to behave. I also need more money and a better home. I want to feel safe and certain in this dream world. I want everything and everyone to be the way I want them to be. Dear God, I have grievances and complaints. Can you please solve them for me? Please?

How can we be at peace when the dominant desire of the ego, which we have identified as us, is for things, circumstances and people to be different than they are? The very desire for things to be different moves us farther and farther away from peace, and therefore seemingly further separated from God.

We are fooled by believing that praying for things to be different will bring us peace. We think if things were different, we would feel peaceful. But we all know that never happens. When a check comes, and we can pay the rent we feel the absence of fear for a short time until the next rent payment is due. A new illness or problem is constantly popping up. We are kept in swirling challenging existence where the best we can do is to keep putting out fires, only to turn around and see another fire burning behind us.

ACIM Lesson 80. Let me recognize my problems have been solved.

If you are willing to recognize your problems, you will recognize you have no problems. Your one central problem has been answered and you have no other. Therefore, you must be at peace. Salvation thus depends on recognizing this one problem and understanding it has been solved. One problem, one solution. Freedom from conflict has been given you. Accept that fact and you are ready to take your rightful place in God's plan for salvation.

ACIM Lesson 79 Let me recognize the problem so it can be solved.

No one could solve all the problems the world appears to hold. They seem to be on so many levels, in such varying forms and with such varied content, that they confront you with an impossible situation. Dismay and depression are inevitable as you regard them. Some spring up unexpectedly, just as you think you have resolved the previous ones. Others remain to haunt you from time to time, only to be hidden again but still unresolved.

To desire or pray to have certainty and safety as a person or a figure in the dream is the desire to be different than we were created. It is the desire for something other than the peace of God. We are Christ. To desire for things to be different than the way they are now is the desire not to be Christ. To place our attention on the desire to change our personal world is the forgetting of who we are. Trust that God knows what is needed in our happy dream and that what is needed will be provided as long as the needed thing does not cause us to delay in the dream.

True prayer includes acknowledging with gratitude that we have been given everything in our creation and letting the Holy Spirit or Jesus take care of all earthly concerns.

We must be willing to trust that our needs will be met by our letting go of our specific desires to the Holy Spirit so that we can re-align with the desire for peace. We can and must let go of the prayer of "Dear God, things are not the way I want them to be."

Please understand that true prayer as described is *not a rejection* of what it is that we think we need. It is not a prayer of "I refuse and reject money for my rent. I do not want a loving relationship. Nope, I don't want love and rent money. I reject that desire."

These are the words that ego has whispered to me many times when I go into silence with a concern or difficulty. I hand the concern over, but often the ego will float the thought that by not asking for money for the rent, or a solution to whatever the problem may be, I am saying I don't want money for the rent or a solution to the problem.

It takes great strength and faith to release what we have come to view as "reasonable requests" of God in favor of desiring the peace of God above all else as described in Lesson 185. Remember that when we desire the peace of God above all else, we are not saying INSTEAD of all else. We are just leaving the "all else" to the Holy Spirit to provide for our best interest. Trusting Trust is so very much the key. Our only "problem" is the belief that we are separate from God, from Harmony. We must learn to trust what we don't see. We must learn to trust the Infinite Invisible. In the words of **Joel Goldsmith (1954):**

Stop making images (of God) in your mind. Stop picturing what God must look like, and trust the Infinite-Invisible, that penetrates and intra-penetrates all being and understand that the Kingdom of God (Spirit) is within you. The place whereupon you stand is holy ground. And even if it seems at this moment in hell, God is right there with you!

The beseeching, the begging of a God that is a father-like male figure sitting on a throne going through our prayers and giving a thumbs up or a thumbs down to each request is insanity. For instance, I ask that my best friend be healed of cancer. At the same time, you ask for your mother to be healed of cancer. And at the same time, probably thousands upon thousands of people across the imaginary globe are praying that someone be healed of cancer.

How in the world does this God figure out who He should heal? Should He only consider prayers if they come from us when we are our knees in a church? How about if we light a candle with the prayer while on our knees in a church? How about if we say five Hail Marys? What about six? Is six "Our Fathers" more effective than ten Hail Marys? How about we just badger this God everyday thinking he will just get so tired of our praying that He will heal the cancer? How about this. This is sure to work. How about we strike a deal, a bargain with God. If you heal my cancer, I will work with poor children and volunteer at a homeless shelter. Bottom line is that religion has created a Santa Claus−like God that grants wishes if we have been good but leaves nothing under the healing tree if we are judged as not worthy of being healed.

So many people have been turned away from the Love of our Creator because of the false teachings of religion and religious prayer. We walk away from churches, religions and God when we feel like God does nothing for us at all. We pray like the church teaches, but it does not change anything. Of course, the ego would have it no other way. You see, the ego, the big fat lie that you are not with God right now and that the appearance-world is real, is also the teacher of this kind of prayer. It is the teacher that nothing is the way it should be. It teaches there is no divine order and we better be afraid of God.

Real Sacred Prayer is the realization of the Presence of the Peace and Perfect Love of God. Praying to feel and remember the Perfect Love of God is the acknowledgment and acceptance that we remain as God, as Love, created us. It is a soft yet determined refusal to budge from this connection and communing. It is the acknowledgment that all is in divine order designed for my highest good, for my awakening back into the eternal peace of Heaven. Prayer is the asking to remember who we are and all that we have been given in our creation.

ACIM LESSON 110 I am as God created me.

If you remain as God created you, appearances cannot replace the truth, health cannot turn to sickness, nor can death be substituted for life, or fear for love. All this has not occurred, if you remain as God created you. You need no thought but just this one, to let redemption come to light the world and free it from the past.

*The healing power of today's idea is limitless. It is the birthplace of all miracles, the great restorer of truth to the awareness of the world. Practice today's idea with gratitude. **This is the truth that comes to set you free.** This is the truth that God has promised you. This is the Word in which all sorrow ends.*

I am as God created me. His Son can suffer nothing.
And I am His Son.

And:

ACIM Text Chapter 4 V

All things work together for good, except in the eyes of the ego.

The corollary to this is that from the point of view ("eyes") of "*I am as I was Created*" is that I was created as Christ and remain as Invulnerable Christ. I choose to remain as I was created. As I was created, I look through the eyes of Love, the eyes of Christ. My point of view then is that all is always in divine order, regardless of what the appearance-world shows me. **My Christ Mind *is* divine order and I have never ever left my Christ Mind. Divine order is that everything works together for good. As we remember and keep this in mind with a soft laser-like focus, Harmony and Peace will begin to take the place of chaos in the dream world.**

The appearance world can, in a sense, change because the appearance world is an effect and not a cause. The "change" may even be more accurately described as a collapsing of time produced by the miracle realization of the Truth. God is the Only Cause. We are His Effect. We must come to accept that it is a dream and it is not real. This doesn't mean we don't see appearances any longer. What it does mean is that we don't see it as real.

Like when we go to Disney's Haunted Mansion. We see the ghosts and goblins, but we know they are not real. And then, with this knowing acceptance as our foundation, we look at the dream movie with the Holy Spirit, the Eyes of Christ, our Spiritual eyes. This is our Real Vision. As we allow ourselves to "see" through our spiritual eyes, miracles happen within the dream. The sequence of dream time shifts. The dream can become more harmonious and peaceful when we let go of this seeing with our human eyes. Sometimes appearances change and sometimes nothing really changes except that we are at Peace even in the face of difficulty. Part and parcel with believing what the human eyes show us is the belief in what it is that is shown to us. This is darkness. This is seeing through a "glass darkly."

What may be considered the most advanced spiritual Truth in *A Course in Miracles* is "Atonement," the Final Miracle. Atonement essentially means that we have accepted that we see a dream world and that it never really "happened." This is the Atonement, or the complete forgiveness or "overlooking" of appearances. So as we become "attuned" to the truth that we never left Home, we "atone," or undo, the dream we seem to see.

Atonement is a core term, a foundation in *A Course in Miracles*. It is important to understand. For me, it took some time for it to gel. Again, the basic definition of Atonement in *The Course* is simply the acceptance deep within that the appearance world of separation from God never "happened" and does not exist.

ACIM Chapter 1 VI 5

Only Perfect Love Exists,
If there is fear,
It produces a state that does not exist.

And also:

ACIM Chapter 2 VI 7

Know first that this is fear.
Fear arises from lack of love.
The only remedy for lack of love is Perfect Love.
Perfect Love is the Atonement. (!)

Perfect Love then, is the Miracle.

There are many passages in the Course that tell us over and over again that the objective world never happened and does not exist;

ACIM Lesson 234 Father, today I am Your Son again.

For today we anticipate the time when dreams of sin
and guilt are gone, and we have reached the holy peace
we never left. Merely a tiny instant has elapsed
between eternity and timelessness. So brief the interval
there was no lapse in continuity, nor break in thoughts
which are forever unified as one. NOTHING HAS EVER
HAPPENED to disturb the peace of God the Father and
the Son. This we accept as wholly true today.

Lesson 132 I loose the world from all I thought it was.

But healing is the gift of those who are prepared to learn that THERE IS NO WORLD and can accept the lesson now. Today's idea is true because the WORLD DOES NOT EXIST. How can a world of time and place exist if you remain as God created you? There IS NO WORLD because it is a thought apart from God and made to separate the Father and the Son and break away a part of God Himself and thus destroy his wholeness.

Lesson 9 I see nothing as it is now.

It is difficult for the untrained mind to believe that what it seems to picture IS NOT THERE.

Text Chapter 26 III 4

Nothing the Son of God believes can be destroyed. But what is truth to him must be brought to the last comparison that he will ever make; the last evaluation that will be possible, the final judgment upon this world. It is the judgment of the truth upon illusion, of knowledge on perception: "IT HAS NO MEANING AND DOES NOT EXIST."

Never happened? Does not exist? What is it then that I am seeing? What are these appearances? What are all those bodies and cars and clouds and stars? The ego, the personal self, the imposter self, says we would have to be nuts to accept this Perfect Love Atonement notion. I can tell you that I struggled with this concept of Atonement. Jesus tells us over and over again in The *Course* that the world is an illusion and does not exist; it's a dream that's over and is not there. Joel Goldsmith says it in all his books. Appearances are a dream and we are mesmerized by its sights and sounds. I wanted to believe it and know it. I wanted to know that I am as I was created by God. So, every day I continued to ask for more proof. I have already been shown in so many ways, so I can now see and realize the divine order of my life. I am able to look "back" on the things that happened in my life and can see the Divine timing of events and people that appeared in my life at just the right moment. I could see the miracles in the extraordinary "happenings." Connecting with Gary Spivey on a radio show on that seemingly random workday. He was a gift who helped open my spiritual eyes. He appeared in cities and a baseball stadium when I needed him.

Jesus appeared at a Hay House convention and then gave me his painting, which has led me to more miracles to even begin to count. He has never stopped guiding and inspiring me. *A Course in Miracles* came into my life just at the exact right moment. Because of it, I helped my earthly father laugh at death and remember that he was not the body. I now teach ACIM, and my speaking opportunities continue to grow.

If we truly want to wake up to the truth, we must keep asking Spirit to show us that the appearance-world is a dream. One of my daily mantras is: *"Love, Show me the truth. Show me. Love, show me who I am."*

The appearance-world continues to challenge us every day. This is not a path of withdrawal. It is a path of faith and fixed determination to "do" everything possible to stay in peace, to stay in the Kingdom of Heaven. I have a family and a law office. Rent, tuition and electric bills need to be paid. Relationships need to be attended to and nurtured. Dishes need washing and clothes need ironing. Unexpected events pop up at the seeming most inopportune time that require time and attention. The appearance-world is unpredictable and chaotic. How we respond to it will make all the difference. Do we choose to know it is not real and Choose the Power of Peace? Or do we respond from the viewpoint of the ego, which encourages us to respond with fear and anger? Choosing instead to *be* the Light of Peace that we *are* will smooth our way. Peace will *literally* arrive at our destination before us when we let it lead the way. We must step back and let the Holiness of Peace walk before us.

If you want peace, you don't talk to your friends. You talk to your enemies.
—Bishop Desmond Tutu

17

VIRGINIA TECH SHOOTINGS

WHEN A MASS SHOOTING happened at Virginia Tech University on April 6, 2007, my daughter Brittney was a student there. It is the deadliest school shooting in the history of the United States. At the time, it was the deadliest mass shooting committed by a lone gunman in U.S history. The gunman, a student at VT, killed 32 people and wounded 17 others.

Brittney is the oldest of my four children. She was the first to leave home and go off to college. In her junior year of high school, she went to visit a friend at Virginia Tech University in Blacksburg Virginia. As a result of that visit, she fell in love with the school and just knew she had to go there after high school. She knew without a doubt that Virginia Tech was calling her name. Sure enough, she was accepted in the late spring of her senior year of high school and spent the entire summer bubbling over with excitement.

At that time, I was able to pull the money together to pay out-of-state tuition, which in and of itself, was a miracle. A few days before school was to start, we loaded up the van and drove from Tampa straight through to Blacksburg Virginia. For those of you who are parents, the moment of dropping off your child at college is a bittersweet moment. Brittney couldn't wait to settle in her dorm and explore the campus. I, on the other hand, knew that I was leaving my daughter a thousand miles away where I no longer would be close by to protect her. That's what fathers do. They protect and guide.

Before I left her to return home, we went to the bookstore to get her books and supplies. My grandfather, Joseph Cardillo, was a Virginia Tech graduate in about 1929 when it was a military school. Brittney and I dug around the massive library collection of old yearbooks looking for his picture. Eventually we found it. In addition to my grandfather, we also found pictures of his brother, who was the first boxing champion at VT. Something about the fact that my grandfather had gone there was comforting for me. Before Brittney decided to go to school at VT, she didn't even know her great-grandfather was a Hokie. She quickly became a Hokie too.

During her second year at Virginia Tech, on April 6, 2007, I was in a hearing in Tampa representing a client for disability. My client, who was in law enforcement, had a sudden and instantaneous spiritual awakening much the same as Eckart Tolle. One day, in an instant, my client woke up in the morning and everything was different. He could see the light and life of God in all things. Colors were vivid and radiant. Sounds were musical. As Jesus would say, in a nutshell, my client could see the Kingdom of Heaven spread out before him. He could clearly hear God's guidance and could feel His Love. My client's spiritual awakening seemed to have been triggered by a very fearful circumstance in his work. Unfortunately, although he was in a very happy, blissful state, he could no longer function at his job as an officer. Years previous, I had represented a train driver who had the exact same experience. Both of these men were divinely led to my law office. Maybe God thought that I needed to understand the experience of these two men. I was able to help them legally, and at the same time they taught me the very real presence of the Kingdom of Heaven spread out before us.

I remember the hearing started early in the morning, and we finished by early afternoon. During the hearing, I felt very much in the Presence of God, because it was clear to me that my client was very literally the focused Presence, and by that time I had learned to step back, let Christ lead the way in all matters and stay in the Light as best as I could. I had read and studied quite a few spiritual books. Some of the most helpful in my quest for peace were Sri Nisargadatta Maharaj, Sri Ramana Maharshi and Joel Goldsmith. But *A Course in Miracles* had become my main focus, although these other teachers played a major role in deepening my understanding and absorption of the Course.

The most perplexing thing to the hearing panel who would decide the issue of disability was the fact that my client was so happy and blissful. Because of this they were unable to understand that deep fear could trigger a spiritual awakening, which is often manifested as bliss and happiness. I could easily understand it. The awakening of Eckhart Tolle was triggered by deep unhappiness and fear to the point when Eckhart said to himself, "I can't live with myself any longer." In that thought Eckhart realized there must be two of him. One was the "I" that was at peace and aware of the other self that was deeply unhappy and in fear. After this stunning recognition, he felt a deep whirling vibration within and fell asleep. The last thing he remembers is hearing a voice that said, "resist nothing." When he awoke in the morning, everything was different. He said it was as if he awoke into a completely different beautiful world. His book *The Power of Now* gives a complete explanation. Eckhart Tolle sat on a bench for a couple years unable to function in the world as we know it. So, I understood my client's identical experiences and did the best I could to represent them both. Unfortunately, because the panel could not understand that my client's bliss could have been triggered by fear related to the particular circumstances of his law enforcement work, they denied his disability. He was just too happy.

When we finished the hearing, I grabbed a bite to eat in the cafeteria before heading back to my office. When I got back, my mother called, sounding a bit shaken. She asked if I had seen or heard the news about the mass shooting at Virginia Tech. I told her that I had been in a hearing most of the day and knew nothing about it. She then told me what she knew and asked if I had heard from Brittney. I said, "No, but I am sure she is fine."

When I said that she was fine, I wasn't guessing or hoping. I *knew* she was fine. At the moment my mother gave me the news, a distinct thought arose very quickly, almost simultaneously as she was speaking. The thought was, "You are of the Lineage of Light; all is well." I could feel a very deep presence of peace. I could not sense any concern or fear within myself. I have to say I wondered why there was no fear or concern when my rational mind seemed to be trying to coax me into fear. The best way I could describe it was that the peaceful "I" of "myself" was dominant. "It" had **dominion.** I now had become aware of the horrific nature of what occurred at VT, but there was no "heat" or "charge" of fear in the awareness. Again, I recall thinking how odd it was that I wasn't concerned. It was as if I was in a light bubble of safety and insulation. This "I" was the Holiness that is described throughout the text of ACIM and the workbook lessons. The powerful Holiness lessons had already become very meaningful to me, and I had made them a daily thought in my tool belt of peace:

ACIM Lesson 38 There is nothing my holiness cannot do.

Your holiness reverses all the laws of the world. It is beyond every restriction of time, space distance and limits of any kind. Your holiness is totally unlimited in its power because it establishes you as a Son of God, at one with the Mind of his Creator.

Through your holiness the power of God is made manifest. Through your holiness the power of God is made available. And there is nothing the power of God cannot do. Your holiness, then, can remove all pain, can end all sorrow, and can solve all problems. It can do so in connection with yourself and with anyone else. It is equal in its power to help anyone because it is equal in its power to save anyone.

*The purpose of today's exercise is to begin to instill in you a sense that you have **dominion** over all things because of **what you are**.*

And:

ACIM Lesson 37 My holiness blesses the world.

This idea contains the first glimmerings of your true function in the world, or why you are here. Your purpose is to see the world through your own holiness. Thus, you and the world are blessed together.

Shortly thereafter, my wife called and said that one of the local news channels had called her asking if Brittney was alright. Michelle had not heard about the shooting, either. Although she was a stay-at-home mom at that point busy with our two youngest children, Phoenix and Kira, she never turned on the TV except for children's education shows. When the reporter called, Michelle had no idea of what she was talking about and told her so. My cell phone then began to ring with calls from reporters. I told the reporters that I was sure Brittney is fine and then politely ended the conversation.

At some point in the afternoon, Brittney called to tell us she was fine. However, she said that she narrowly, and miraculously, missed being in or near the shooters path. She explained that when her alarm clock woke her up that morning to go to class, she hit the snooze bar and fell back asleep and ended up missing her class, which was in building near the shooting. Brittney was a reporter for the Virginia Tech newspaper, so her name was available on the AP wire. As a result, she spent the day doing interviews and answering questions from reporters from around the United States.

This explained how the local media was able to locate us in Tampa as a parent of a Virginia Tech student. During dinner that evening, our doorbell rang. When I answered, I was greeted by a local television reporter and cameraman who wanted my comments on the shooting. The reporter asked me a question designed to evoke a response of fear and emotion from me, but I had none to give. I recall silently asking the Holy Spirit what to say. I then told the reporter my daughter was fine and that I was fine, too. I smiled and then politely told them I had nothing else to say.

What is the point of this story? Holiness. The Power of Holiness. The Power of Peace that is our Holiness. The Choosing of Peace and Holiness. Perfect Love.

When we commit to change our purpose in the dream-world, we are essentially replacing the dream purpose of threat, fear and death with the Holy Spirit's purpose of holiness, love and peace. We are making a Sacred Choice, a commitment to remember our own Holiness and see the world appearance through our Holiness. We are committing to see *from* the Holiness point of view that we are in the Reality of Perfect Peace. The Holiness of our Christ mind is our Real Identity. When we look from Holiness, we only see our Holiness. We see the Holiness of our Christ Mind.

I remember the exact moment in my life that I made this commitment. A few months into my divorce in about 1996, the mental, financial and physical strain became overwhelming. Although I ultimately obtained custody of my young daughters, the stress and strain of the whole process was taking its toll on me. One day at lunch, I sat in the small chapel of a church in silence, just looking for some relief and peace. No one was there except me. I just remember feeling fear and pain, not from the ending of the marriage, but rather from the deep confusion and disillusionment of having trusted in the illusion of the "happily ever after" world and then the attendant stress and struggle of detangling from so much negativity. And so, in this state of mind, instinctively, these words came from within me in deep surrender;

"God, unto You I commend by soul."

After these words came out, I sat silently for a few minutes contemplating the peace that followed. I could feel a subtle shift within me which felt like a lifting of weight. It wasn't a dramatic shift, just a feeling of relief, like a removal of a burden. I wondered about the words that I chose. Or more accurately, I wondered where these words came from. I had not thought to sit down and say these words. Rather, when I sat in the chapel that afternoon, I had reached a point where my human mind could no longer process the confusion and chaos. I could not make sense of anything, and I had nothing to grip. My trust in world happiness and in church teachings hit a brick wall. I know now that I had reached a deep point of surrender. And from this deep place of surrender, these words came forth on their own, *"God, unto You I commend by soul."*

The only familiarity I had with these words were related to Jesus, when on the cross close to the death of his body, according to the Bible, he said these words. In my deep surrender and inability to find a stable place to stand, it was these words that cried out from my soul. Now, looking back, I know that it was my Spirit, Christ, the Real me, asking for release from this world of misery, insanity and pain. That day in the chapel was a turning point. There was a recognition that I was no longer in charge of the dream that I had substituted for the Love and Presence of God. I know this now, but I did not know it then.

You see, this dreamlife that we have hallucinated is designed by the ego--the separate personal mind that we chose to believe in. The purpose of the hallucination is to block or veil our Awareness of Tranquil Peace of Heaven. My ability, as a pretend human being attempting to have my own dreamlife as a man in a dream-world, had reached a crisis point. Thank God. I have learned that because we are perfect Spirit, the stress and struggle of pretending to be a limited human body with a personality of likes and dislikes, at some point, will simply be too difficult to maintain.

ACIM Text Chapter 2 II

*You can temporize and you are capable of enormous procrastination, but you cannot depart entirely from your Creator, who set the limits on your ability to miscreate. An imprisoned will engenders a situation which, in the extreme, becomes altogether intolerable. Tolerance for pain may be high, but it is not without limit. Eventually everyone begins to recognize, however dimly, that **there must be a better way.** As this recognition becomes more firmly established, it becomes **a turning point.***

It is kind of like telling a lie. Once told, we have to continually be diligent about covering up the lie with other lies. We have to work at keeping a lie a lie. Then lies create fear. And fear creates defenses and more fear. We have to work and struggle to maintain the appearance that a lie is true. Not so with truth. Truth simply rests in itself. The false has to work at convincing itself that it is true. This is the world that we live in. It is false. We have to stop the lie of pretending that God is dead. We pretend God is dead by our looking away from the Light to the dark dream world that we have adopted as our home. Along with this tragic self-misidentification, comes sickness, poverty, violence, deception and death that are inherent within the belief of the ego hallucination world. The belief that I am a body and can be a helpless victim has been accepted into our mind so that we can be preoccupied with being at the mercy of the world so that we don't remember our divinity, peace and joy. We have become so focused on survival in the dark dream that we have no time to be aware of the Light we are.

We are the Prodigal Son. We have indeed wandered far from Home, far from the Truth. It has become too difficult to maintain the lie. The Virginia Tech shooter's social media revealed that he blamed the world for his actions. He was treated unfairly by the world in his eyes. "You made me do this". He then likened himself to Jesus being crucified on the cross. During his insane attack, he **chained locked** one of the doors to the building so that no one could get in to help or out to escape. This is the voice of the ego:

ACIM Text Chapter 27 I The Picture of Crucifixion

Whenever you consent to suffer pain, to be unfairly treated or in need of anything, you but accuse your brother of attack on God's Son. ***You hold a picture of*** *your crucifixion before his eyes, that he may see his sins are writ in heaven in your blood and death, and go before him, closing off the gate* (**chaining the door**) *and damning him to hell.*

The solution to the mad insanity of this dream of fear and death is to awaken to the Love that we Are. How? *Forgiveness.* Not forgiveness as we learned in the dream world. For in the dream world, the part of us that agrees with the ego's thought system, first concludes that the person or circumstance has indeed done us wrong. The other person or circumstance has been unfair, guilty, mean and unloving. But even though that is the case, I will be the better person and forgive. I will find you guilty, but I will overlook it this time because I am innocent. This is how the false ego world forgives.

The forgiveness that Jesus teaches us in *ACIM* is that it (whatever the "it" maybe) never happened so there is nothing to forgive. We forgive what our brother *did not do.*

If you are depressed you are living in the past, if you are anxious you are living in the future, if you are at peace, you are living in the present – **Lao Tzu**

18

INVEST IN PEACE

JESUS TALKS ABOUT what he calls the Atonement as the real forgiveness. The Atonement is the understanding and acceptance that the dream never happened. The Atonement is the acceptance that only Perfect Love Exits. We want to attune to the Truth that only Perfect Love exists. Like tuning the piano to play the note as it was originally created to play. We are the note of Love, played in the key of Peace.

Atonement is simply our acceptance that only perfect Love exists and that we are out of tune with this One Truth of who we are as God created us. Our out- of-tune-ness began when we seriously entertained the thought of "I wonder if there is more than Everything? I wonder if I can pretend to be different than what I am"?" And from that thought of wonder, sprang the world in which we seem to be slaves to "getting more" in a false appearance and false identity world of scarcity and limitation. This dream world, or really

236

more appropriately, nightmare world, will always be limited and scarce. But of course, the world won't come right out and tell us that. If it did tell us that, we would quit working at it to make it better. It is set up to encourage us to believe that happiness can be found in the dream world of "getting more of" as long as we keep working at trying to fix it.

This appearance world of pretending to be what we are not is the world of what is commonly known as the world of duality, or the world of opposites. This is a world of two-ness. The world of more and less. The world of feeling good and not feeling good. Good days and bad days. Male and female. No money and lots of money. Beautiful people and ugly people and on and on. This world is predicated on opposites and therefore its underpinning is conflict. Opposites conflict. Period. They fight each other for supremacy.

The world we see is designed to inspire and require us to strive for more. More money, more peace, more drama, more happiness, more sex, more thrills, more experiences, more beauty. And on and on and on. The more we get the more we want. It's never "enough". We never reach fullness and completeness. We never have and never will reach peace within a false made up world of opposites. As soon as we have a president Obama, we then have a President Trump. You see? There is no answer in the dream world because opposites are never at peace.

For just a second, think about this. Stop. And think. And realize. What is the motivation for wanting and striving for more? Is there ever a point when we say, in this appearance world, "I have enough". With very rare exceptions, the answer is no. The exceptions are those that have been on a spiritual path of awakening and have a glimmer of realization of the Truth. Which, in a nutshell, Jesus would say, "seek first the Kingdom of heaven, and all else will be provided". What he is essentially saying is to put our awareness on the Presence of Peace, and what is needed, even in the dream world appearance, will be provided without struggle and anxiety and fear. This is the Power of Choosing Peace.

Wanting more of something is not a peaceful feeling. Don't kid yourself about this. Take something as simple as our everyday jobs. In this nightmare dream world not created by Love and Peace (God), we go to university and graduate schools so that we can make money at a job or profession. Many of those jobs and professions can seem to be quite noble and can help relieve pain and suffering. I am in one of those professions a lawyer, at least in the areas of law that I mainly practice. I call it "street law". It's the type of law that a man walks off the street into my office and needs help with a notice of eviction or disability because of a severe illness. Many of the doctors, teachers, nurses, mental health therapists, clergy and first responders, are in helping professions and seem to be motivated by the desire to help. But if we take a close look at this, however well-intentioned and altruistic certain professions and jobs seem to be, the real motivation is to *not to be aware of God by pretending to be a something we are not.* Even this world "doing good" is part of the false world of duality.

But the good news is that once we become aware that our original intention was to substitute our work for the presence of God, we can re-purpose that same work or profession to be used by the Holy Spirit to awaken ourselves and those we touch. We can now be used by the Holy Spirit in the best way possible for the benefit of all concerned. We surrender the control and direction of our work into the hands of the Holy Spirit and Jesus and let Christ do all things through us right where we are.

Doing "good things" is better than a poke in the eye with a red-hot poker, but it is still part of the dream of duality. The of doing good things and deeds offsets the doing of bad things. And so, in the dream world miserable game of opposites, we are fooled into believing that we can defeat, or at least, beat back the bad and evil in the world. When all the while, it is all a hallucination we made up in our mind and we fight the good fight. We struggle to make it. We dig deep and persevere. And we struggle with nothing but our own dream.

We have to give credit to the dream world of earth. It's very convincing. Very enticing to see a wrong that needs to be righted. An illness that needs to be cured. A knight in shining armor has come to rescue the princess. A doctor or a lawyer or a President, arrives and declares "I can fix this"! And then we get to play the hero in a dream we made up with made up problems of sickness and scarcity. Again, this is better than intentionally trying to cause pain and misery. But even our best efforts at helping are simply a temporary band aid unless they are done with the guidance and presence of the Holy Spirit. Yes, we need to reach out a helping hand to those who seem to need help. Yes, do this. But know that we are working within a dream world and it is now our intention to work with the Light of the Holy Spirit to awaken ourselves and those around us. Then as we do this "good" work within the dream, we do it with the awareness of the Presence of Christ as our real identity and as the real identity of those we appear to help. Without this awareness of the Truth of our Identity of Christ, we remain lost in the dream world fighting and struggling, never realizing, and therefore not escaping, the world of fear and scarcity.

Years ago, after I had taken a deposition in a downtown Tampa high rise, I had a few minutes to sit in the beautiful lobby on the ground floor that was decorated with leather chairs and giant paintings. After the deposition, which as I recall was pretty much a waste of time, I sat in the lobby just to take stock of the frustration of the fruitless pursuit of what I thought of as the "good fight".

As I sat there in the lobby I looked up, and right in front of me was a life-sized statue of Don Quixote on a horse waving his sword. It took me a while to understand the symbolic message I was being shown. At the time, I remember going over the Don Quixote story in my mind. The story of fighting battles and enemies that turned out to be hallucinations or illusions, symbolized by his doing battle with windmills as though they were mighty enemies. When really, there was nothing there to fight. And so it is with the world that we seem to live a life in. We wave our swords at a non-existent enemy. The enemy is non-existent because anything that was not created by God is not Real and has no True Existence. It, the problem that is pictured in our dream world, has a false existence in the sense that it is a "thought" that out-pictures. The presenting "problem image" is a thought that is of the ego or personal self. And the image or picture wants us to take it seriously and swing our sword at it for our whole dream life. Then the body dies, and we dream of another hero dream body story in an effort to not wake up to the Presence of the Peace of our Christ Self.

All of this appearance world is the out picturing, the image making, of our thought of "I wonder if there is something more than the peace of God. I wonder if there is something more outside the gate of heaven." And out of this thought was the whole dream world of war, death and chaos made.

ACIM Lesson 15 My thoughts are images I have made.

It is because the thoughts you think you think appear as images that you do not recognize them as nothing. You

*think you think them and so you think you see them.
This is how your "seeing" was made. This is the
function you have given your body's eyes. It is not
seeing. It is image making. It takes the place of seeing,
replacing vision with illusions.*

**ACIM Lesson 23 I can escape the world I see by giving
up attack thoughts.**

*The world you see is a vengeful world, and everything
in it is a symbol of vengeance. Each of your perceptions
of "external reality" is a pictorial representation of your
own attack thoughts. One can well ask if this can be
called seeing. Is not fantasy a better word for such a
process, and hallucination a more appropriate term for
the result?*

Let's say you love going to Las Vegas to play the slot
machines with the hope of winning the jackpot that will
give you a life of ease. There you are, with thousands
of people around the world on any given Saturday night,
from Monte Carlo to Las Vegas, sitting there dumping
money into a machine and yanking on a handle in hopes
that your troubles can be solved with your winnings.

While you are playing, dumping dollar after dollar into
the machine, a man walks over and sits at the machine
beside you. You then notice he begins to talk to the
machine in a very lighthearted way. You lean in a little
to hear what he is saying.

"Hey, we have done this dance before, you can't tempt me to invest in this world of uncertainty and risk. I know it's rigged. You want me to believe that you, a man-made machine, can make me happy. And you, the machine and the owners of this casino, try to convince me I can find real happiness here by allowing some people every day to win while diverting attention away from all those that lose everything. You want me to believe that I can win too. You, the machine made by the casino, create the illusion that wants me to keep coming back for more." Then man says, "I have seen through you, overcome you and I am here now to help others to see the lie of this made up illusory casino world."

The man then turns to you and looks directly in your eyes. You don't turn away, because there is something there that feels familiar. There is something in his eyes that you know. He asks you to trust him. He asks you to take his hand and let him lead you from the casino of winning and losing. You are hesitant. Why would I want to leave here, you ask yourself? It's kind of fun really. There is a chance I could win enough money and then I would be happy and content for the rest of my life!

This man, who apparently is a mind reader, asks you to give an accounting of your wins and losses. Very quickly, you realize that you have been coming to this casino for years and years, lifetime after lifetime, but you have never ever won. Yes, a few dollars here and there. But you realize you never have left the casino

243

with a gain. Just as quickly, a voice in your head reminds you that you keep coming back because there is a chance at happiness and contentment. You have listened to that voice because it sounds quite logical. People around you seem to be winning and happy. Not everybody, but the voice tells you that you have a real shot at it. It's possible. You have tasted a little success here and there. Yes, yes, the voice says, sure there have been defeats. But you are determined to find happiness and contentment so pay no mind to setbacks. Happiness is here, you just have to keep pulling the handle.

You have listened to this voice for years now, encouraging you that happiness is just one pull of the handle away. Now this man next to you is encouraging you to trust him and get up and walk out of the casino with him. He says its rigged. He says it is all a set up. He says there is no way to win here in the casino. It's a fantasy meant to keep you hungry for more. And it knows how to play on your weaknesses to keep you coming back, to keep you hopeful that happiness can be found here.

As you take a breath and look around, you see what you have tried to deny. The thought has crossed your mind before. The thought that this casino is rigged and that you have never really won here. Yes, that thought has crossed your mind many times. That voice, though, keeps encouraging you to come back. In that moment you realize that you have been coming back because there is no alternative. There is only scarcity and sickness and general chaos out there in the world. You realize that you feel like you have no choice but to ignore the obvious futility of trying to win in the casino. It's better to pretend you are happy and hopeful rather than to face what appears to be the alternative of giving up in the casino world. Keep pulling on the machine, the voice says, just close your eyes and ears and keep pulling.

Now this man, with such peaceful eyes and sincerity, is asking you to trust him. He says his name is Jesus. But you know Jesus left this earth a long while ago. You remember that story in the Bible about the Shepard that will always come looking for his lost sheep. In that instant you remember him and his promise. In that moment you decide to surrender because you have grown so weary of not finding happiness and contentment within this world. You take his hand and trust him.

He smiles. With his hand firmly wrapped around yours, you feel his strength and resolve. He knows what he is doing, and you feel it. The two of you arise from sitting in front of the machine and you head towards the door. As you get closer to the door, you realize its not the door you came in through. The door then begins to fade and is replaced by a bright white radiant light. Jesus looks at you to assure you that you can step into the Light with him by your side. The Light seems familiar and inviting.

As you are about to walk into the Light, Jesus stops, winks and says there is something he forgot to do. "Wait here," he says, "I will be right back".

You watch him walk over to one of the roulette tables. He gently asks everyone to step back. And after they have done so, and without the slightest bit of anger, he flips the table over, markers and coins flying in all directions.

He then returns to your side, smiles, takes your hand and walks you into the Light.

Attain His Peace and you will
remember Him.
–ACIM

19

THE POWER OF CHOOSING PEACE

WE ALL HAVE THOSE MOMENTS of not knowing what to do and being afraid of making a wrong decision. We don't want that feeling of making a "wrong" choice and then later feeling regret. This fear of "what may happen" in the future pervades every nook and cranny of our lives. This threat is always present. We may try to deny and cover it over with lots of money, activity, drugs and alcohol, but "it", the threat and fear of the unknown tomorrow, lurks beneath the surface of our mind. The ego encourages us to pacify this fear about tomorrow in various distracting ways. The ego keeps us focused on the future unknown purposely **so that we don't ever realize the eternal infinite peace that we actually exist in and as right here right now in this present instant. The Peace of God is the only Power that exists. It is here *now.***

ACIM Chapter 27 III 7. Beyond All Symbols

A Power wholly limitless has come, not to destroy, but to receive its own. There is no choice of function anywhere. The choice you fear to lose you never had. Yet only this appears to interfere with Power unlimited and single thoughts, complete and happy, without opposite. You do not know the **Peace of Power** *that opposes nothing. Yet no other kind can be at all. Give welcome to the* <u>Power beyond forgiveness</u>, *and beyond the world of symbols and of limitations. He would merely be, and so he merely is."*

The ego does not want us to *Know Only Peace*. The ego, the false sense of a personal self, is absolutely okay and fine with us knowing **about peace, which is different than Knowing Peace.** The ego is all too happy to have us curiously look at the concept of peace as if it were an exhibit at a Museum of Fine Art.

"Yes, yes it says, that's a very fine rendition of this attractive concept of peace. How soothing it looks. That painter sure knew what he was doing. What talent. What a remarkable gift he has to be able to show us the concept of peace in all those colors. Just wonderful! Don't you think Jack, it's just so beautiful! I shall buy it. I don't care how much it costs. Jack, we are rich and have more money that we need. Can we buy it Jack? I want to go see the curator right now and find out how much it costs. Let's go Jack, let's go right now!"

Jack and his wife met with the curator that very afternoon. The curator's name was Mr. Smith. Jack and his wife, Jill, didn't like him so much. Very mysterious man, with very little personality and a forced smile. Jack and Jill just wanted to buy the painting entitled "Peace" and be on their way.

Mr. Smith seemed pleased that they wanted the painting, after all it was so full of beautiful peaceful colors and seemed to convey the idea of peace. He could understand their desire to own it. He explained that it was a very valuable painting and that it was only to be sold at a very high price.

"This is one of a kind. It is for a very discriminating collector. The price is one million dollars", said Mr. Smith. He then turned and looked out the window at the city streets below.

Jill said yes most emphatically. Yes, they would pay one million dollars for "Peace".

Mr. Smith did his best to act surprised that people could be fooled into believing that "Peace" could be purchased. He had thousands of years of experience in dealing with people looking for peace and he was so very willing to sell it. Mr. Smith also knew that the the Real Painter of "Peace" gives it freely to whomever asks. It is not for sale and can certainly never be purchased. This Prince of Peace, the Painter, has nothing to sell. His peace is given freely to those who ask.

But the experience of Mr. Smith through the centuries has been that people have a most curious notion that peace can be purchased with money. After all, Mr. Smith was there when the pyramids were built to pacify and bring peace to the rulers in the blood of the workers. Mr. Smith was there during the Inquisitions that were going to bring peace to the Church. Mr. Smith has been there during the thousands of wars and slaughters that have plagued the planet in the name of peace. Wars are mainly about money, land and resources. Mr. Smith knows that and through the years, he has convinced the world that peace can be purchased with money in the form of guns, tanks, bombs and war planes. If a nation or a church has money, soldiers can be paid to kill. And everyone knows that killing and attack for land and religious belief brings world peace.

As he spoke to Jack and Jill, a smile came across his face as he realized that they too had fallen into the trap of believing that peace could be purchased. It is so easy to attract people to peace. Just make it beautiful and colorful. Mankind will want to possess it at any price. Sometimes peace looks like a beautiful beach or a splendidly decorated New York apartment. Just keep the deception hidden in the squint of the radiating beauty. Paint the exotic car in alluring metallic with lines that draw the mind to imagine owning and driving it. Own this car and you will be at peace. How happy you will be! Look at that gorgeous woman, or that handsome, rich man. Wow, if I could possess that, I would be so happy, I would be at peace!

Mr. Smith has made a lot of sales over the years and now he was about to sell a painting called "Peace" to Jack and Jill. By the end of the day, Jack had wired one million dollars to Mr. Smith who immediately called his assistant to his office on the top floor of the museum. He instructed the assistant to go to the basement storeroom and pull out the painting of "Peace". But the assistant informed Mr. Smith that they had run out of copies of "Peace" that they had been selling.

Mr. Smith explained to his assistant that one that was just returned and was available. "Some guy returned it and didn't even want his money back. He is a man who I sold peace to years ago. He is a lawyer and says has he has no need for false peace. Said something about peace can't be found in this world, and at any rate, certainly can't be bought. This guy also mentioned book called *A Course in Miracles*. I said I never heard of it and sent him on his way. Curious fellow though, reminded me of that guy Yeshua a few thousand years ago that I tried my hardest to sell peace to. You remember, all he had to do to buy his peace was to admit that when he said that he and God were "one", he really didn't mean it. I showed him the attraction of avoiding a tortuous death with a simple admission. But he didn't buy it. He should have, because he just ended up crucified and then a religion sprung about him that teaches that peace is purchased through suffering and sacrifice. I tried to warn him, but he refused. This lawyer that returned the painting sure seemed to admire that Yeshua character. I wonder what he knows.

Anyway, go get that painting of "Peace" that he returned and clean it up. Deliver it to Jack and Jill this evening so that they will be at peace."

Later that evening, the delivery truck delivered "Peace" to Jack and Jill. They happily hung it in their private gallery, so overjoyed that they had purchased peace. Every evening they pour a glass of fine red wine and visit "Peace". They are so pleased to look at it and know every color and brush stroke. Sometimes they have guests and tell them all about "Peace" and what a beautiful painting it is indeed.

When everyone has left, the lights are turned off and the door to "Peace's" gallery is shut tight. The alarm is set, and "Peace" is safely hidden away. Jack and Jill don't sleep very well though. They worry "Peace" may be stolen. Jill often gets up in the middle of the night to check the locks and the alarm. Mr. Smith knows she won't sleep at night and will never be at peace. Even he knows that real Peace cannot hang on a wall or be kept in a bank account or be driven on the street. Mr. Smith knows that peace is within each Soul. He knows that the Creator created only peace. Mr. Smith knows that if people found that out, he would be out of the job of selling a false sense of peace. Mr. Smith knows that Jack and Jill know all *about* peace, but they don't *know* peace. Mr. Smith also is realizing that Yeshua is still teaching people to KNOW PEACE. Mr. Smith will soon have nothing to sell.

And so, as we steadfastly refuse to know anything but peace, the ego will dissolve. That means that anxiety will dissipate. Depression will lift. The iron bands around the mind will loosen and snap off. All of mankind lives in varying levels of anxiety and depression, all of which inspire frantic activity in an effort to make the fear and anxiety go away. As is often the case, the more money one has access to, the easier it is to distract oneself by engaging in endless activities to keep the mind from experiencing the anxiety. Excessive shopping for stuff we don't need and excessive trips and travel are another. "Always on the go", is a favorite attempt to escape the peace filled present moment.

We are all familiar with the Bible quote that says:

"Be still and know that I am God."

I have a large wooden plaque with these words on my bookshelf. It reminds me ever so gently to remember God's Loving Presence in the midst of the busy day. My guess is that most people reading this book don't sit on a mountaintop somewhere looking down at life from afar. Most of us are actively engaged in the world. We have jobs, children, significant others, parents and bills to pay. We have worldly "responsibilities" that cannot be glossed over or suddenly abandoned when we come to understand that the world that seemed so real is imagination and that we are not the body. *A Course in Miracles* teaches us to view the life that we are living in a different way. The different way of living is in the way we look at it or view it. *A Course in Miracles* encourages us to see or view our world from another perspective and with another teacher sitting by our side teaching or instructing us about what we are seeing and how to interpret the scene. The teacher that sits with us watching the movie about what seems to be our life helps us understand the meaninglessness of the scenes we are watching. It is a dream movie of fear and anxiety. Jesus and the Holy Spirit represent the Power of Peace that is our Holiness. From that perspective or viewpoint, we can learn to remember to see with our Holy Eyes, and all things will work together for good.

ACIM Lesson 38 There is nothing my holiness can not do.

Through your holiness the power of God is made manifest. Through your holiness the power of God is made available. And there is nothing the power of God can not do. Your holiness, then, can remove all pain, can end all sorrow, and can solve all problems. It can do so in connection with yourself and with anyone else. It is equal in its power to help anyone because it is equal in its power to save anyone.

If we retreat from the world and go find an island or mountain top where there is an absence of worldly activity, there likely would be more awareness of inner peace. I have meditated for 25 years or so and have been on meditative retreats that are helpful experiences. But always, after that 30-minute meditation in the morning, or after the 2-day retreat, the world calls us back to duty. Clients to represent, bills to pay, children to raise and relationships to nurture.

That's why I am fixated on bringing *A Course in Miracles* to the street level. What does that mean? It means that my particular way of explaining ACIM is mainly by demonstration and by stories either from my life or someone's life that the Holy Spirit can point to as an example to bring the material and the teachings of this most sacred book to light. There are many places in ACIM that Jesus flat out says that this *Course* is meant to be practical. It is meant to actually *be applied* to our life, to what is going on right in front of our eyes. This is critical to convincing ourselves that we are entitled to miracles.

Jesus is in no way advocating or encouraging us to abandon our earthly dream lives. He does not tell us that the world is an illusion and full of misery and suffering and then tell us to deal with it by going to a mountain top in the illusion. When one gets to the mountain top, one is still in the illusion. It's just a mountain top in the illusion. Sure, absolutely find quiet places to withdraw now and then. Yes, that is fine and very helpful. But don't believe that we can escape to a "sacred" place here in the earth dream. Temporary escapes to peaceful landscapes, mountains and beaches can be rejuvenating temporarily. Just recognize anywhere where we "go" in the dream is always an illusion. The place we get to, the mountain top, does not exist. Certainly, the quietness of the forest or the cathedral can be conducive to contemplation, but so can sitting at a kitchen table in Brooklyn. Or sitting on a picnic table in a city park.

In the **ACIM Workbook for Students, Review I,** Jesus says:

*"It will be necessary, however, that you learn to require no special settings in which to apply what you have learned. You will need your learning most in situations that appear to be upsetting, rather than those that already seem to be calm and quiet. The purpose of your learning is to enable you to bring the quiet with you, and to heal stress and turmoil. **This is not done by avoiding them (unpeaceful situations) and seeking a haven of isolation for yourself.***

You will yet learn that peace is part of you and requires only that you be there to embrace any situation in which you are. And finally, you will learn that there is no limit to where you are, so that your peace is everywhere, as you are."

This is where the rubber meets the road. Every day I do my best to keep this in mind. This situation, this problem, this relationship issue, this financial issue, this legal issue, this child issue, this work issue, is where the rubber meets the road. The *"this"* we are dealing with is where the rubber meets the road. It is an opportunity for us to apply the Course lessons and teachings to the person, situation, event or problem at hand. The teachings and lessons from ACIM can be likened to a brand-new set of Pirelli tires on our car.

These new tires grip the road at the highest speeds and in the tight corners. These tires are designed to hold a firm grip on a wet road. We can trust them. They are designed for extreme driving through unexpected twists and turns of the street.

In the same way, *A Course in Miracles* was designed to handle the twists and turns of the dream world. The "rubber" is the *Course* and *Workbook*. The Lessons and the Text are to be trusted and applied to the issue at hand. We can count on the Truth in ACIM to take us safely through tight corners and high-speed problems. Every day, our life is like a wet, twisting high speed highway. Problems and situations fly at us quicker than we can think. But an experienced driver knows his tires will grip.

One who trusts Jesus and his words in ACIM, has the "tires" that will absolutely hold the road, no matter the magnitude and multiplicity of the challenges to peace that constantly arise in our day in day out lives. The lessons are lessons of peace and healing for our mind so full of twists and turns of fearful imaginings.

Over the past twenty years or so, I have been as vigilant as humanly possible in applying the lessons to what comes up during the day. Our daily life, although dream, is the proving ground for the Truth and Truth's effectiveness upon our feelings of fear and conflict that we all face every day, to one extent or another. We should not fool ourselves into believing that life *isn't so bad.* Rather, apply the Lessons. We must stop trying to

handle problems and issues the way we always have.
Hand them to the Holy Spirit and Jesus. We need the
Help that can see beyond what our physical eyes see.

ACIM The Song of Prayer

*You child of God, the Gifts of God are yours, not by
your plans but by His Holy Will. His voice will teach you
what forgiveness is, and how to give it as he wills it be.
Do not then seek to understand what is beyond you yet,
but let it be a way to draw you up to where the eyes of
Christ become the sight you choose.* **Give up all else,
for there is nothing else.**

As we deepen our trust that we are Christ, every single
one of us, we begin to dislodge from our minds the false
notion that we have separated from Perfect Love. This
journey is all about regaining our awareness of our
Identity as Love, as Christ. We sweetly gently
surrender unto our Creator, as we simply start each day
with this prayer:

"Love, show me the way. Love show me who I am."

Remember, always remember, that what is going on
right in front of us, what is appearing to our physical
eyes are pictures that we dreamed up. They are in our
mind and they are all past and gone. What comes up as
our lives in the dream is over and therefore *not there.*

Text Chapter 28 I Present Memory

The miracle does nothing. All it does is undo. And thus it cancels out the interference to what has been done. It does not add, but merely takes away. And what it takes away is long since gone but being kept in memory appears to have immediate effects. This world was over long ago. The thoughts that made it are no longer in the mind that thought of them and loved them for a little while. The miracle but shows the past is gone, and what is truly gone has no effects.

All the effects of guilt are no more. For guilt is over. In its passing went all its consequences, left without a cause. Why would you cling to it in memory if you did not desire its effects?

I know the *"not there"* part, the *"does not exist"* part of the Course's fundamental teaching is a bit difficult to wrap our minds around. But what God did not create is not real and does not exist. Period. We find the words *"does not exist"*, *"is not there"* and *"is not real"* repeated over and over again. Obviously, this phrase is repeated so often because it is critical to accept. The importance of this acceptance is crucial to remembering and allowing the Peace of God to flow and resolve all conflict.

Lesson 132 *I Loose the world from all I thought it was.*

__There is no world__! This is the central thought the course attempts to teach. Not everyone is ready to accept it, and each one must go as far as he can let himself be led along the road to truth. He will return and *go still farther, or perhaps step back a while and then return again. But healing is the gift for those who are prepared to learn there is no world and can accept the lesson now. Today's idea is true because the <u>world does not exist</u>. And if it is indeed your own imagining, then you can loose it from all things you ever thought it was by merely changing all the thoughts that gave it these appearances. The sick are healed when you let go of all thoughts of sickness and the dead arise when you let thoughts of life replace all thoughts you ever held of death.*

Jesus would have us remember that the journey is over and that we can view it from a point where it has ended. The dream of guilt is finished. It is no more. It is done, having never really happened in Truth. The dream of death flashed across the mind for an instant, then disappeared into the nothingness that it was.

God Is. Only the Truth is True, and nothing else is true. There is nothing else but Truth, Love, Joy and Happiness, all encompassed in God's Eternal Peace. There is nothing else. Trust that the Power of *your* Choosing Peace, will bring you through the Gate of Paradise, to play happily for eternity in the green Lawns and Meadows of Heaven.

ACIM 24 V

"The sight of Christ is all there is to see. The song of Christ is all there is to hear. The hand of Christ is all

there is to hold. There is no journey but to walk with Him."

Come now and abide in God's Perfect Peace, Perfect Love and Perfect Holiness. It is here that I wait for you.